The Builder's Companion
BOOK 2

START BUILDING TO CERTIFICATE OF OCCUPANCY
US/Canada Edition

Manage and Build Your Home

PHILIP FITZPATRICK
A Builders Companion Series

Copyright © 2021 Balcombe Bay Publishing

All rights reserved. No part of this book may be reproduced, stored in a retrieval system or transmitted, in any form or by any means, without the prior written consent of the publishers, except in the case of brief quotations, embodied in reviews and articles. This publication contains the opinions and ideas of its author. It is intended to provide helpful and informative information on the subject matter covered. It is sold with the understanding that the author and publisher are not engaged in rendering professional services in this book. The author and publisher specifically disclaim any responsibility for the liability, loss or risk, personal or otherwise, which is incurred as a consequence, directly or indirectly, of the use and application of any of the contents of this book.

ISBN 978-0-6450958-0-7 (paperback)
ISBN 978-0-6450958-2-1 (e-book)

Published by Balcombe Bay Publishing. BBP

Also by Philip Fitzpatrick

The Builder's Companion
Book 1
Zero to Building Permit
US/Canada Edition
Your Complete Guide to Home Building

The Builder's Companion
Book 1
Zero to Planning Permission
UK/Ireland Edition
Your Complete Guide to Home Building

The Builder's Companion
Book 2
Start Building to Completion Certificate
UK/Ireland Edition
Manage and Build Your Home

The Builder's Companion
Book 1
Zero to Planning Permit
Australia/New Zealand Edition
Your Complete Guide to Home Building

The Builder's Companion
Book 2
Start Building to Occupancy Permit
Australia/New Zealand Edition
Manage and Build Your Home

and published by Balcombe Bay Publishing BBP

Kickstart Your Project

Download Your FREE Bonus!

Scan the QR-code to access the

*The Builder's Companion
Schedules and Charts Workbook*

SCAN ME
https://abuilderscompanion.com/get-your-free-ebook

Download
*The 1-Page Building Plan
Schedule of Works
The Players Chart
Project Milestones Chart
What Does it Do?
Build Cost Projection Budget
Good Practice Check Box
Defects (Punch) List
Finish Schedule*

TABLE OF CONTENTS

Acknowledgments vii
Introduction ix
The 1-Page Build Plan xv

Chapter 1   Things You Should Understand 1
Chapter 2   Project Management 15
Chapter 3   Health & Safety 39
Chapter 4   How to Finish 55
Chapter 5   Start Works 65
Chapter 6   Building Codes 83
Chapter 7   Excavations 91
Chapter 8   External Infrastructure and Home Services 99
Chapter 9   Site Works – Below Damp-Proof Course (DPC) 119
Chapter 10   Works Above Damp-Proof Course (DPC) 143
Chapter 11   Fit Out 171
Chapter 12   Making a 'Good Deal' 187
Chapter 13   Alternative Dispute Resolution (ADR) 207

Conclusion 213
Women in Construction 215
General Glossary 217
Abbreviations 223
Services Abbreviations 229
Excavation Glossary 231
Professional Roles 233
Index 241
About the Author 243
Take-Aways 245
Do you feel 'Companionable'? 249

ACKNOWLEDGMENTS

Building is a team activity as is producing a book. Many people lend a hand and this is of greater benefit than they know. Their advice and the experiences they shared are greatly appreciated.

Books 1 & 2

Reviewers
Brendan Hoban	Founder, Hoban-Hynes, Melbourne Australia.
Alan O'Doherty	Lawyer & Realtor, Sotheby's International Realty, New York & Connecticut USA.
Paul Browne	Solicitor, London UK.
John Boecker	Architect, Author and Environmentalist, 7group / Boecker Consulting Services New Jersey USA.
Peter Hammond	Author, London UK.
Mark Fitzpatrick	Builder & Services Engineer, London UK.

Editor
Jennifer Lancaster   Power of Words, Brisbane Australia.

Architectural sketches
Pam Toan   Designer, Hoban-Hynes, Melbourne Australia.

INTRODUCTION

'If there was only one solution to every problem, the world would be insanely dull'.

– Kara Barbieri

Are you attempting the Everest of challenges: to build your own house on time and within budget? All the endless possibilities can seem overwhelming, but with the guidance here hopefully you'll feel empowered to make decisions. The purpose of this practical book is to help you as Owner-Builder whittle down your options and assist you to confidently give instructions.

The Builder's Companion comprises of two books. Book 1, Zero to Building Permit, introduces the stages and decision-making processes to be considered and acted on before building your new home. Planning and preparation must be rigorous to get the best result from your owner-build project.

This book focusses on all the things an owner-builder must know to build a modern, environmentally-sound home. It's best to be read while you're gathering information on home building and are becoming clearer on direction, but well before an on-site plumber asks you where a pipe should go!

Why are you building a new home or renovating an older home? There are many homes that are for sale in all conditions and styles and in all areas. Some owner-builders want the challenge and some want to be able to create their own home with their own hands… some just want a better house for less money. No idea is more worthy or important than any other; what is important is that you are committed to the project.

I have built homes and numerous other buildings around the world all my working life and sometimes feel that I have seen everything at least once! This is of course not true and we are always hearing of new ideas and building techniques. The world around us is changing fast and our homes become a mirror to this change as well as a response. Home-builders must design in the spaces and comforts that society has come to expect and we must, even when building a single home, respond to global challenges.

It is easy to believe that this is all for other people to concern themselves with. But if you want to meet ever tightening building regulations and codes, or will ever look to sell your property, then you must build in a manner that is aware of the expectations to only sustainably develop. In the-not-too distant future, a premium price will be paid for sustainable homes and a price drop for those needing retrofitting. It is always more expensive to upgrade a building than to construct it sustainably from the beginning.

The two books are part of 'A Builders Companion' series with the 'companion' part being the most important. The books are an aid for you to rely on and must be relevant to you as an owner-builder. There are innumerable technical points of information available on the internet, but the internet does not bring all the parts together to a single point. That is the role of the 'companion'.

First, let's review the processes of planning and purchase.

Plot purchase comes after discussions with consultants but before briefing consultants.

Securing a suitable plot for an as yet un-designed home is a real chicken-and-egg situation. You need answers to confirm your instinct to purchase, and yet you cannot get definitive answers to many questions over design and cost. Architects/designers/lawyers can at least advise on site suitability and try to tease out if it is suitable for your family needs.

When considering the purchase of a plot, you will be concerned as to its current zoning and planning status and will want to be confident your home designs will receive a building permit.

There are other practicalities too. Have you ensured all external boundaries are correct and rights do not extend to others over access and egress? Legal limitations are always followed by financial implications and so you must ensure you are at the right end of any deal.

Even before the brief, even before the purchase, you must be able to assure yourself that the whole project is financially feasible. At this stage, some questions to ask are: Have I allowed sufficient costs? and, what items should be included? What information do I still need to collect?

After purchase, matters are more serious and all major decisions affect all other decisions. Are you going to employ a builder or owner-build? How much emphasis must you place on project management? What tactics will you employ to meet the demands of building a fine home on time and within budget?

You will need a team of consultants, so who will you appoint? What can they do for you and how much will you need to budget for their fees? Do you need a consultant planner or can the designer take this role all the way through to the issue of a building permit?

It is important you consider all available options – along with the design direction you wish to go in – before you agree a program with your design team. For example, what do you think about ecological features, or say, the merits of timber cladding versus aluminum? How large a home would you prefer to build?

If you're up to the design program point, are you ready to discuss it? Which stages of the design will you achieve before agreement and freezing the scheme? Are all areas equal or do some have more functions than others? What are your planning professional's major responsibilities? Who are the other players affecting your design that you do not employ? Are these players committed to your project?

The program is a distillation of the vast range of options and opportunities available to you and points you in the direction of the intended size and style of the home.

The finished house will be a reflection of its owners; the choice of what it is and how it is built is one available for you to grasp with both hands. Building a home is not a passive option but in fact is one of the most exciting thing you can ever do!

> **TIP BOX**
>
> *Murphy's Law*
>
> Murphy's famous law is often termed as 'anything that can go wrong, will go wrong'. It is almost as if a mythical force takes over just to ruin whatever you are trying to achieve.
>
> There is another law, called the Samuel Goldwyn law, which states, 'The harder I work, the luckier I get'. This can be amended for the owner-builder to be 'the better I manage, the luckier I get'. As regards the owner-builder, things generally go wrong at certain stages. By effectively managing these stages, opportunities to mention Mr. Murphy decrease.

Murphy Avoidance Stages

Stage 1: Design.

- Have a clear overall design to be shared with those who need it.
- Listen to your consultants and contractors.
- Carefully look at overall designs and identify cross-over points between trades.
- Prepare larger scale details or written notes to cover these crossovers so people are clear on what to do.
- Within a trade, is there a certain way you would prefer something arranged? An example is: which specific lights you want connected to which specific switch. If so, make sure you communicate this on a drawing.
- Indicate routes you want services and drains, etc. to follow. This can be within the house or externally.
- Spray paint large numerals indicating datum levels spread across the site. This relates specified heights back to your build levels.

Stage 2: Site Organization.

- Keep a clean site.
- Materials are to be stored neatly and safely.
- Meet all Health and Safety (OH&S) requirements.
- Laminate copies of current drawings on site for reference.

- Tell everyone who will listen that you are pleased to discuss any points of the work they may not be crystal clear on.
- Repeat clear instructions to ensure the listener 'gets' your message.
- Update the schedule of works regularly.
- Keep in touch with contractors on site and those scheduled to attend.
- Keep in touch with suppliers and be across delivery issues.
- Be clear on what items of work need to be checked or certified as part of the building control process.
- Listen to what people are saying.
- Be a good neighbor.

Stage 3: Office.

- Keep a clean set of approved building permit drawings.
- Drawings and specifications are to be available as hard copies and electronic copies.
- Confirm all material orders in writing (electronically will be OK).
- Keep and file all delivery notes.
- Keep and file all receipts.
- Place all contractor orders in line with the decided contractual process.
- Personally, approve all invoices before payment.
- Prepare only high quality documents for your lender.
- Update costings regularly.
- Update cash flow regularly.
- Keep all warranties and product information in good order.

Things may still go wrong even if you follow up on each and every point listed… but Murphy's Law will have a much larger impact if you do not!

Introduction – Action

- Discuss your build in detail with your designers
- Learn the drawings and details
- Remember Occupational Health and Safety
- Draw up a Schedule of Works
- Cash-flow

THE 1-PAGE BUILD PLAN

How to Use It

Continuing on from The Builder's Companion Book 1, Zero to Building Permit, this Book contains a proposed outline for The 1-Page Build Plan, as a general overview. As before, this is not meant to be your Build Plan but more to show how it may look once you have started.

The construction of your own home can often become all-encompassing and as your personal project it is never complete, but rather always a work in progress.

The 1-Page Build Plan indicates the various stages of the project and how you may break down the items in the 'big picture'. Throughout the chapters are updated sample 1-Page Build Plans that reflect issues that typically arise through the build process. These go into much more detail but are only for guidance. The purpose of the exercise is that you name your own headings and identify key points. This system will chart your course through the project. How much micro detail you go into is down to personal preference. This assists you to recognize if you need further information on what is 'coming over the horizon'. 'The 1-Page Build Plan' should act as a prompter of what you need to address.

The idea is to break down tasks in a logical way and have an overall visual diagram of what needs to be done. When items are achieved, they can be highlighted or deleted, to be replaced by upcoming issues.

MONEY
Budget & Cash Flow
Finance Timings
Sign Off Financial Agreement

TEAM
What Enabling Works Need To Be Done?
Prepare The Team To Start

DESIGN
Review Planning - Do You Want What You Have Got?
Seek Quotations
Instruct Working Drawings
Building Control Approval

PLANNING
Discharge Planning Conditions
Confirm No Further Applications Needed

TIME
Set Start Date & Update Works Program

GENERAL
Identify Contractors

CHAPTER 1
SUMMARY

Once you have a building permit for your project, it's time to consider all the technologies you should include.

Highlights covered in this chapter include:

- What is net zero carbon?
- Low energy designs
- Heat pumps
- Coefficient of Performance
- Smart Home Technology

CHAPTER 1

THINGS YOU SHOULD UNDERSTAND

'Everyone hears only what he understands'.
– Johann Wolfgang von Goethe

Owner-Building is a journey, but nothing like an actual journey. When travelling, you pack your suitcases and whatever was packed is what you end up with on arrival at your destination. Whereas when you first consider the owner-builder journey you know certain details, perhaps what you would like to accomplish, but other details are either unthought of or unclear. These details come into focus during the owner-build experience, many not even in your original 'suitcase'.

Through a drawn-out process to plan what you wanted, you acquired a plot of land, engaged professional consultants, agreed a design, achieved planning permission, secured finance and are now seriously in place to commence the construction of your home.

Before you start building work, there are things you should know about in general, and if a topic is of interest to your build, then you should investigate it in greater detail. (Many of these themes are covered in more depth in The Builder's Companion, Book 1 and in later chapters of this book.)

The perfect starting point is for all the topics below to be considered and investigated fully, prior to seeking a building permit. That way, relevant technologies are incorporated as part of your original design. However, things are rarely perfect and often the process is a very busy one and usually only so many features were considered. You have a chance to think 'outside of the box'. It's an opportunity to make the house even more special by considering the topics included in this chapter and reviewing what is *in* and what is *out*.

The world view of climate change is rapidly shifting and it's widely agreed global warming has created a global crisis. New housing should reflect this new stance including the methods of construction selected and the features incorporated. It is generally agreed that during a new building's lifetime, days will on average be warmer than in past years and there will be an annual increase in the number of very hot days. The carbon dioxide atmosphere concentration is higher today than ever before and bears a constant relationship to fossil fuel burning.

What Does Net Zero Carbon Emissions Mean?

Every person has an individual carbon footprint. This 'footprint' is the amount of greenhouse gases caused by this person's activities. As well as everyday living, by cooking or growing food, buying clothes and traveling, we all directly or indirectly cause greenhouse gas emissions.

Each person's emissions are totalled and the country's behavior on land use, fossil fuel, power generation, etc. are added to the mix to provide the country's total carbon footprint. This is expressed as tons of Carbon Dioxide – CO^2. By adding together all countries' emissions, you get the global tons of CO^2 we humans are producing.

So how can we help effect change in our build? *Net zero carbon emissions* means removing other carbon emissions to match the carbon emissions your efforts are creating. As well, there are many opportunities to select green products or particular designs in your new home to reduce your family's carbon footprint. The manufacture of building materials accounts for about 11 percent of the total CO^2 produced in the world. You can help by checking the materials' green status and purchasing products which have taken a lower level of CO^2 to manufacture and deliver to site. There are also opportunities to help by planting gardens and by having green roofs or ponds to absorb carbon emissions.

> **TIP BOX**
>
> Why ponds? Research in the US has found small-scale ponds are excellent at burying carbon. The ponds are super-effective as their carbon capture rate is 20 times more efficient than trees. Small ponds also work at a higher rate per ft^2 (m^2) than large ones. Plus, you can take enjoyment from knowing you are encouraging wildlife as well as helping the atmosphere.

Governments all over the world are introducing legislation to reduce the carbon footprint in all parts of the construction process. You may feel you only need to comply with principles of carbon reduction as far as the government has legislated at the time of construction.

Most commercial builders up till now adopted this same viewpoint and did the minimum works to comply. They felt that the whole business was an imposition and another barrier erected between them and completion. A change in public attitudes on energy efficiency and sustainable design are rapidly occurring and the realization of the benefits of protecting our direct environment has taken place. When you market your owner-built home for sale at a future time, you may well find people do not wish to purchase traditional designs and energy-wasteful spacious homes. Rather, the opposite view will in all likelihood be popular. Purchasers will increasingly look for highly insulated homes powered by renewable energy sources.

Ener Guide for New Homes (EGNH) is administered by the Canadian government which is similar to the US House Energy Rating Scheme (HERS). They both promote smart well-built and energy efficient homes. A rating system awards points for the highest specification houses when compared to the national construction code.

Low Energy House Designs.

Many across the world are moving towards 'low energy housing' or sustainable designs. There is no single form of low energy design. These are houses designed to use natural resources, with little environmental impact during the construction process. The aim is to operate the home in an energy efficient manner, with minimum fossil fuel usage. These designs minimise changes to the occupant's lifestyle and let them enjoy their home without increasing their carbon footprint. Discussion and designs are based on the following:

Passive Solar Design.

Through design, it's possible to control and direct the heat entering through the building's well-insulated fabric and openings, and at the same time, reduce the temperature by directing cooling airflows. This means naturally, without electrical and mechanical means. The aim is to achieve indoor thermal comfort without using fossil fuel-sourced energy.

Your geographical location has a bearing, yet the principle of *a heated home with little or no energy used to heat it* is the gold standard of the passive house.

As these homes must be well-insulated and airtight to achieve this outcome, a system allowing fresh air must be installed. Air intake should be managed by drawing from the cool, shady side in hot weather and the warm, sunny side in cold weather and exhausting in the opposite direction. Cool air is dense and falls down and warm air rises, and this principle can be utilised to drive your system.

Active Solar House

Active Solar Design.

These are designs incorporating passive solar collectors and linking them to mechanical and electrical power sources to boost their efficiency and delivery. By making them active, the solar panels improve energy efficiency and more than compensate for the power used by their operation. An example is a solar array hot water system with pumps to greatly increase the amount of water circulating and receiving energy from the sun.

To maximize solar advantage; a few experimental houses have been built on turntables so that they rotate to track the suns position during the day. This approach is seen as a novelty now but perhaps this will become a future trend.

Mechanical Services.

Heat pumps take heat and transfer it from one place to another. In effect, they can take heat from air, water or soil and transfer this heat into your home. As heat pumps don't use fossil fuels to create heat, using these pumps allows you to heat your home from natural renewable sources. Heat pumps can provide warm air or work in reverse and provide cool air, and some systems provide domestic warm water. Depending on circumstances, they can either achieve the required heat temperature themselves or be topped up by other means to meet heat requirements.

The most common heat pumps are:

Air Source Heat Pumps (ASHP). These pumps use external air as a heat source, by treating external air and transferring it to heat the interior of the home. ASHP's can also operate as a cooling system during the warmer seasons. To understand the process they are if you like a reverse refrigerator, taking cold outside air and providing warm internal air. ASHP's are cheaper to install than GSHP's although as ever budgets should be looked at across the whole of the project.

Ground Source Heat Pumps (GSHP) aka Geothermal. The earth is a heat sink, absorbing heat from the air and the sun. It generally lags about six months behind the seasons, so it is warm in winter and cool in summer. Earth-linked heat exchangers using water or air can capture this resource. Pumps can be connected to pipes drilled down into the earth to depths of 100-500 feet (30-150m) or circle horizontally around a larger earth area at a depth of say 5' 0" (1.5m).

Water mixed with antifreeze circulates through a loop, collecting heat from the earth. This mixture is pumped through a ground heat exchanger and supplies either a heating or cooling system. The system takes heat out of the soil during the winter season or returns heat during the summer season.

A further variation is to install a heat plate into a body of water, an adjacent river or dam and take the heat from the water. A minimum depth of 6' (1.8m) is required throughout the year.

By predicting the entering water temperature (EWT), a smaller and cheaper heat exchanger may be suitable for purchase, as these only need to top up already-heated water.

You should investigate if heat pumps can 'reasonably' heat and cool your home without a back-up heating/cooling system. The answer will be dependent on where you are geographically located, the size and design of the spaces to be heated and how much is financially reasonable. The heat pumps' efficiency can be assisted by your selected design and levels of insulation. By creating an airtight building envelope, you can more accurately predict heat demand as you can rely on heat loss calculations. By calculating an SAP (Standard Assessment Procedure) rating, you can produce a predicted energy assessment. Unplanned ventilation will cause your house to under-perform and your calculated insulation levels to be inadequate . Ask your local energy consultant for guidance.

Coefficient of Performance (COP) aka (CP).

COP is a useful guide to how efficient your designed system will be. The principle is: the electrical energy to run the system should be less than the energy the system delivers. This is expressed as a ratio that is arrived at during the design process. If your system provides 4 units of energy and takes 1 unit of electrical power to operate the system, you have a COP of 4.

For a Ground Source Heat Pump, a reasonable COP ratio is in the region of 3.5 to 4.5 and an Air Source Heat Pump (ASHP) should have a COP of 2.0 to 3.0.

Domestic Water / Hydronic Heating.

Domestic water can be connected to the GSHP either directly or indirectly. Directly, by connecting a water storage tank and taking the heat to energise a domestic water service or a hydronic water central heating system. Or indirectly, through a smaller, secondary heat exchanger called a desuperheater. This configuration is the more common one. It can be very effective and increase hot water efficiency while reducing costs.

Mechanical Ventilation Heat Recovery (MVHR).

MVHR is a system of conditioning air within the rooms of a building by mixing previously heated or cooled air with fresh incoming air. This comprises a core unit and piped channels for fresh and exhaust air, which are pushed around by blower fans. This system significantly increases efficiency and reduces heating costs.

There are a few system types and they are able to cross over or act alone. Again, selection will very much depend on the design and house location. The MVHR can be incorporated in a ventilation unit joined to a heat pump and ground exchanger.

MVHR installations are best designed and calculated by an engineer and are very effective at reducing heating costs. They also provide planned fresh air, as opposed to accidental air circulation through unplanned drafts.

Gray Water Recycling / Water Management.

Gray water recycling is the second use of water within the home. Care has to be taken as 'dirty' water can spread disease. But by thinking through how water can be reused, it can lead to a more efficient use of a resource. At its simplest, collect safe gray water by bucket and disperse over the garden. Be aware of bleaches and chemicals as they can be problematic to plants. This is efficient, non-mechanical and free.

By treating the gray water, it can be used to flush toilets or re-run through the washing machine to wash clothes. It can be sprayed by hose or drip irrigated onto the garden.

A managed approach is to install tanks to capture rain water. This can consist of a garden rain barrel connected to a down-pipe or a system of collection from different gutters to a centralised storage tank. Stored water is fed by pump to a garden hose bib or perhaps used intensively, such as swimming pool re-filling.

Do not use gray water for human or animal consumption.

Smart Home Technology (SHT).

Technology making chores easier has been going on for centuries. The speed of change and practical use of AI and digital technologies is, however, having a profound effect on what is normally used in the home.

Smart technology is now about making our home life more pleasant and labor-saving. A robot sweeps and vacuums your rooms; it can work out where the stairs are, to avoid a tumble, and reverse up. This is a time-saving gadget and perhaps a health improver as it will relentlessly track down dirt and suck it up.

Technology has to be accommodated into the furniture design or it will not function properly. Robotic vacuums cannot operate under chairs if they do not fit under, so all new sofas or armchairs must have legs that lift the base up by a minimum amount.

In this case, the assistance you get through technology will result in less choice in the chair market. This is just an example of technology unexpectedly changing other design elements of the home and reducing your options.

The opposite is also true, where products can have extra programs added after purchase. An example of this is washing machines that allow you to download extra wash functions and settings from the internet should the standard choice not be sufficient. So, SHT can bring drawbacks and restrictions as well as wider choices; this is the way of progress.

SHT can also take care of dangerous or awkward tasks by including technological assistance. An example is remote-controlled electric motors which can open high-level windows at night in summer. This will ventilate the room; hot air trapped within the house can find an easy path outside. This can be further improved by fitting a rain and wind sensor to automatically close the windows during inclement weather.

These days, a Wi-Fi connection is a basic requirement and as a minimum, it must work anywhere in the home. Your provider and your region's connections will be crucial.

Many people find home security gives a sense of safety. The alarm monitors your home while you're asleep, when you're at work and when you're not in the country, giving you peace of mind.

Security systems range from the simple intruder alarm reacting when a door is opened, to sophisticated installations monitoring room air movement (and burglar movements). These can be watched over by professional monitoring services or linked to camera systems at the house. These cameras can show each zone to the homeowner wherever he is in this connected world.

Doors can be remotely opened for delivery or tradespeople and security systems monitor and record who entered, where they went and when they left. Keys may be becoming a thing of the past, with fobs opening doors and recording entry. Even this has been superseded by fingerprint and iris operated locks and reduced touch point systems that work by your mobile phone scanning a pad. The world of locks and keys is rapidly changing.

SHT increases energy efficiency too. Smart thermostats are linked to the system and closely monitor different room temperatures and overall system performance. You can view a small screen which links to a meter. This meter, for example, sets washing machines/dishwashers running when sufficient energy is produced by PV panels harvesting solar energy. Using your home-produced energy saves you buying more expensive energy from the grid.

A smart home can also be of tremendous assistance to persons with special needs. By remote control or voice accessing technology, you can put things in motion; from closing blinds to changing the music on a 'smart-speaker' or summoning help. It may appear to be a gizmo to a person without special needs but it can be life transforming for others.

To win in the world of technology, you must dedicate time to understand which technologies you are accepting into the design and how you will use and adopt them. By understanding better, you can feel in charge rather than overwhelmed.

Energy-Saving Landscaping and Low-Maintenance Landscaping.

Landscaping of the garden areas is not often mentioned in relation to owner-building. Yet the garden can be an ally in energy saving and if you can also make it low maintenance and attractive, this is a win-win. Even keen gardeners who enjoy puttering about in the garden. can find other exciting gardening jobs if the basics take care of themselves.

Start by consulting charts and books covering plant hardiness in your area and consider appropriate plants and trees. Selecting the best plants and trees for your plot and planting them to maximize solar gain in winter months and solar shielding in summer months can save energy and cost.

Before planting, consider your land's latitude and the shadow a large tree will create. Be careful not to shade solar panels as this will reduce their effectiveness. To this end, do some simple research on how much shadow the midday sun will create at your location. This information is readily available by sun calculator apps on the internet.

Create natural shading by planting small to medium trees, shrubs and vines. In summer, this will reduce the ground temperature around your home. In winter, it still allows the sun in to warm your home. Plant deciduous trees closer to the house as they lose their leaves in winter to let the sun through and regain leaves in summer to shade the home. Evergreens can be planted further away, to protect from winds during the winter. Be aware of tree root systems, which may damage your foundations, and how tall the trees will become when fully grown.

Urban Heat Islands (UHI).

Across the USA, Tokyo, London, Sydney, and many other cities, 'Heat Island' policies are being adopted by city authorities. It was realised that dark-colored roofs and roads can greatly increase local temperatures.

The New York Cools Roofs initiative has led to roofs all over the city painted in a reflective white finish which according to NASA has reduced the white roof temperature by 42F (23C) over its unpainted dark neighbor. This was estimated to have produced savings of 2,282 tonnes of CO^2 per year. The City of Los Angeles reduced surface road temperatures in the region of 10/15F during the summer by painting roads with a white sealant.

What can you do to reduce temperatures?

- Select trees to give canopy shade to gardens and houses.
- Install reflective or light-colored roofs and roadways.
- Minimise energy use, especially at peak times.
- Conserve and maximise vegetation.
- Water Sensitive Urban Design (WSUD) – install water recycling and keep vegetation damp and watered.
- Reduce personal car use.

The End Game

For many people, the 'end game' is to build a home for themselves and their families. This is a good goal but things do change and sometimes you have to change with them. Thinking of the future, you are best served to maximize your options. If your house is saleable and you are in a position to move, then all well and good. If it is otherwise, then stress and financial loss may occur.

It is my belief that in the future, 'green' perceptions will take hold. You do not want to be selling an analogue television in a smart television world. Retrofitting is invariably more expensive, and with some elements, nigh on impossible without major demolition.

For instance, how can you change single glazing to double or triple glazing without a new window? How do you stop *cold bridges* from outside to inside without taking down serious parts of the structure? The time to consider high levels of insulation and effectively seal the building so it is air-tight (with planned mechanical ventilation with heat recovery) is *before* construction, not after.

You must consider how things may change in the next few years. Many people, over many years, have predicted things that have just not happened but what have we already heard about that is coming down the line? For example, if you live in an urban area will you be receiving packages by drone? If so, should a 'drone delivery hatch' be built in? I have not yet seen the specification for such a hatch but it is worth asking the question.

You should consider all these items and pursue the ones that appeal to you and your family. Discuss various options you all liked with your key designers to see what should be included and what will require a varied building permit submission.

In the end, you will occupy your home and enjoy the fruit of your labor… but a 'smart' approach could be the way to go.

Chapter 1 – Action

- Are you intending to make changes to the approved design?
- Find out if you formally need to amend your building permit approved scheme
- Review your current selections and consider if a more environmentally appropriate choice can be made

MONEY
Budget & Cash Flow
Finance Timings

WORKS
Survey And Set Out
SWMS

TEAM
Clear Site And Start

TIME
Update Works Program

DESIGN
Is a PQS (CE) On The Team?
Seek Quotations

GENERAL
OH&S In Place Or Planned
How 'Green' Is Your Home

CHAPTER 2
SUMMARY

Project Management is the fundamental skill of the owner-builder. This is the skill to keep all the balls in the air while meeting financial commitments.

Highlights covered in this chapter include:

- Monitor/Plan, break down tasks, Goal Gradient
- Access digital information anywhere, anytime
- Understanding risk
- Scope/Reduction Creep
- Develop a critical path

CHAPTER 2

PROJECT MANAGEMENT

'The only place where success comes before work is in the dictionary'.
— Vidal Sassoon

The owner-builder needs project management skills over and above every other 'named' skill. Let's review which skills belong to others.

A consultant will bring imaginative solutions and improve how you look at your build project. They will advise on good practice and ensure the designs are within the building codes and regulations.

A tradesperson has to bring a high quality of expertise to the works within their skillset. They must manage their material ordering to ensure the correct products/materials and quantities are delivered and available to use.

A site manager has to fuse the designs he sees with materials and skilled labor to create a structure. He must be prepared to talk to all the 'trades'; he'll discuss points of the heating system and then swap straight into kitchen fitting or window installation.

The overarching process is management of the whole project. The managerial action has to be transformative; it must take plans and turn these into productive powerhouses. This will come together by uniting labor, material, plant, knowledge, regulation and finance.

In your manager role, ensure you have a procedure of how you pass on revised design details to contractors. Record when contractors are issued with the latest updates and take old versions away from site. If this becomes part of your usual routine, it is more likely to be consistently done.

Champion.

The project manager is the champion of the project. He or she cares about all aspects of the finished project. This is a commitment from the beginning to the end. It is imperative that someone taking on the build of his own home is tuned in and involved in all the major and minor decisions. They must know what their goals are and what the aim for the project is. They must have both tactics and a strategy to get them collaboratively to the finish line.

Tactic.

Consider the input you get from your consultants and designers as raw data. This means design, regulations and codes of practice… and how this must be put together. This information input is mixed in with the style and content of what you want to include in your home.

Strategy.

The output from all this is a smooth information flow, which is then to be provided to contractors and operatives. They simply want relevant information and instruction, allowing them to efficiently progress their works. This is provided by drawings, specifications, schedule of work and clear instruction.

Collaboration.

The combination of the strategy and tactic brings you to collaboration. This is what you work towards: everyone in the larger team working in the same direction with the same aims.

To do this, the information you provide must be fully complete. If there is a detail change, this must be communicated and recorded. With modern technology, this information should be available digitally and accessible anywhere, any time.

The Process from Raw Data to Final Build

Personnel + Logistical + Financial (PLF).

The project manager must take the approved plans to an actual piece of land and direct many, many individuals with thousands of items of material to come together in a common purpose. To this end, the three major thrusts of the strategy are personnel, logistical and financial.

The PLF points must all unite to construct a physical structure to a high standard. The organizer does this by co-ordinating the labor, equipment and materials. This is not an easy task, as you are overseeing the building of a one-off design at a one-off location, despite the weather, unforeseen issues, and anything else thrown at it; all to be completed to meet a fixed budget.

It can be that the major decisions are easier to make than the minor decisions.

The following are examples of the types of decisions you must make.

A major decision could be the selection of the type of foundation. The minor decisions set the narrative of the house. How tall are the internal door openings designed to be? What door furniture is selected? Is there room and finance available for a built-in coffee machine as part of the kitchen design? The coffee machine is perhaps whimsical, but the minor decisions set the tone and are noticed.

The minor decisions come into play as part of the imaginative decision-making process and are drawn out by the program. You start with the ideas to include features to make the home special and you need to be organized enough to bring these ideas to fruition.

Before a decision is made to change something, you must determine if this item has a cost or time delay. Once the decision to vary the works is taken, the information continues on in the circular process *from raw data to build*. The starting point for all decisions are one of the following:

- Occasional
- Periodic
- Continuous

Occasional.

This is information picked up irregularly or when it happens. This could be information of which you have just become aware. An example could be an unforeseen ground condition. Worryingly, this can raise a cost issue. Is it something you can design around or is it a crucial part of the build process? You will need to make a short-term decision, which may affect budgets in the long term. Can you cover the cost from your contingency fund? Whatever the effect, the overall schedule and cash flow will need to be updated and further decisions made.

Periodic.

This is information continuously collected and reported on at regular intervals. Your lender will want updates before they release further funds, so they will instruct a surveyor to report on your progress and provide a valuation. The surveyor will accept input from you and you generating updated schedules of work indicating site progress, will be very useful to both of you.

This provides the lender with your written review of works commenced and completed on site. This sets the scene for the valuation. Supply a brief application, stating how much you consider the drawdown should be. The surveyor will review these documents and recommend a value. This information is incredibly useful to you as it crystallizes how well (or otherwise) you are doing and gives you an opportunity to make changes.

Continuous.

You continuously create information on site.

Which tradespeople did you instruct? What materials were delivered? When will outstanding invoices become due? What orders do you wish to place and when will these become due for payment?

Specific items to watch are those covered by any type of lump sum, prime cost sum or provisional sum. If you allowed an amount for general labor during the whole build, how are you getting on in the midst of the project, as a percentage? Will this amount be exceeded?

Also, rubbish removal… how many refuse dumpsters did you budget for? How is your estimate working out? Often, at the finish of a build, waste seems to exponentially grow.

From this, you can see that a system of costings is crucial. These pieces of information should periodically be added to the cash flow chart and become part of your regularly considered information.

Set Up.

The next requirement are the tools to oversee and deliver the project to completion.

The site needs to be set up and able to deliver. You need to decide on site security, facilities and organisation.

Security.

Are you going to secure the building area boundary? This is decided by location. If you are located in an urban area you should strongly consider effective construction fencing to keep out uninvited visitors. Everyone walking on your site is your responsibility, as detailed in Chapter 3.

Are you leaving tools and equipment on site when the site is closed overnight or at weekends? How will these be kept safe from theft? Secure storage can be the answer or removing all tools and plant at the end of each day. Whatever the answer it should be a thought through decision and not just an evolving situation.

Office and Site Facilities.

What on-site facilities are you required to provide in your area?

Find out the minimum site conditions you need to provide for a working construction site and consider upgrading. Commonly a working site toilet, handwashing with warm water facilities and a cold drinking water tap are supplied. Basic kettle and coffee/tea facilities and somewhere to take a break in relative comfort. This can all be provided by hiring portable cabins that are fitted out for these purposes. You only pay for the weeks that the cabins are on site. You could also benefit from an office area but here your particular situation will come into play.

Protection.

Protect special features such as trees and bushes that are to remain after the works are complete. Hi-visibility plastic tape and fencing can be cheap and effective. Protection can be a condition of the building permit and is an easy fix to comply.

First Aid.

Strongly consider attending a First Aid course so that you can provide basic First Aid should an accident occur. Purchase a kit that contains all the recommended bandages and plasters and you will be confident that you comply with requirements. This can be considered as part of your training and preparation.

Project Manager.

The next requirement are the tools and people to oversee and deliver the project to completion. Part of the make-up of a good manager is a calm and collected manner. The Project Manager must be able to negotiate with anybody, and it could be between people and/or organizations. If you need information to progress works, you may need to get involved to solve the query. This creates a 'can-do' attitude and team-building naturally follows on. A positive consequence of this style can be to move attitudes forward to a higher level of productivity. People like to be part of a team and so they react well to a positive attitude. The Project Manager sets the rules and keeps to them. For example, if you wish to have a high visibility workwear and hard hat site, you must lead from the front and always be dressed safely and appropriately.

Planning

It is good practice to breakdown your overall site schedule of work into individual trades or items of work. All plans are better when focused on goals. Work should be set to commence and complete at specific dates and keep careful track of progress.

TRUE STORY

Lead-in Times

I was once tasked to place an order for Italian marble cladding for a multi-storey building's large external elevations. Placing the order in a foreign

> language was okay, after we got through the approval process for the cutting drawings and even designer approval after his visit to the quarry in Italy. Every piece of stone had to be individually approved and was to be cut, polished and made to measure.
>
> I naïvely assumed the cutting and polishing process for Italian marble would take place in Italy. The stone was shipped to Brazil but not before getting stuck in Italian customs on the way out. Customs issues were repeated on arrival in Brazil. On completion of the process, on the way out of Brazil, we again had customs issues.
>
> The suppliers and manufacturers in both countries had worked to their timescales but international bureaucracy had intervened. This caused a major delay, leading to works installed out of sequence as a way to maintain progress.
>
> Always check lead-in times for any and all special orders… and then check again!

Schedule of Work.

A Construction Methodology chart (*Program of Work or a Work Schedule*) can be: a simple list developed into a bar chart, or a complex chart with interactive, digital links on it. The basics of both are the same. The success of the document is dependent on the information included.

For a single owner-built home, the items need to be co-ordinated but can be kept quite simple. As long as you monitor and regularly update this document, it will serve you well.

First, list in sequence the construction operations. This is done to recognize the completion point. This can be detailed or broad brush, depending on your enthusiasm and skill level. The greater the detail included, the more accurate the emerging picture will be.

Try not to be too precious about the exact sequence at this stage. This will change as the information is sifted and compiled. This will, at a minimum, list the targets you are to achieve.

PHILIP FITZPATRICK

List of Tasks	Wk 1	Wk 2	Wk 3	Wk 4	Wk 5	Wk 6	Wk 7	Wk 8	Wk 9	Wk 10	Wk 11	Wk 12	Wk 13	Wk 14	Wk 15	Wk 16	Wk 17	Wk 18
	1-Nov	8-Nov	15-Nov	22-Nov	29-Nov	6-Dec	13-Dec	20-Dec to 02-Jan		3-Jan	10-Jan	17-Jan	24-Jan	31-Jan	7-Feb	14-Feb	21-Feb	28-Feb
Reduce levels / Pile Topsoil								\multicolumn{2}{CHRISTMAS}									
Excavate Foundations																		
Drainage																		
Concrete Foundations / Slab																		
Timber Frame / External Covering / Roof																		
External Brickwork																		
Fit Windows and Doors																		
Internal Walls																		
Electrical Installation																		
Heating Installation																		
Plumbing																		
Drywall																		
Concrete Driveway																		
Smart House Wiring																		
Fit Out Carpentry																		
Fit Out Bathrooms																		
Install Kitchen																		
Worktop Templates / Return to Fit																		
External Works																		
Smart House Fit Out																		
Painting																		
Tiling																		
Install Appliances																		
Defects List																		
Certification																		
Completion & Snagging																		

Notes:

The schedule should be drawn up to meet your life choices

The reasonably shortest period that a contractor could plan is approximately 12 weeks - Owner builders often schedule up to 52 weeks

You can schedule a master programme and break items into shorter timescales

Deadlines and Goal Gradients.

You can boost perseverance and improve your ability to focus on specific issues if you create deadlines. A deadline can give you stress or it can give you encouragement. If you set an order that objectives should be carried out in and have the self-discipline to work towards these self-imposed deadlines, it can bring real benefits to you and your project.

If instead you look at the enormous mass of things you need to achieve in no defined order, then you may well jump from one activity to the next without a plan. A schedule of order allows you to feel comfortable with not achieving certain items first, since you know you are achieving milestones. Milestones which are all taking you in the right direction. This motivating power is termed 'goal gradients'.

How does this work? As you move towards achieving a goal, you feel a surge of excitement/pleasure. You have successfully reached an important point. You sense you are progressing towards completion. By breaking down the objective into a number of identifiable and measurable tasks, you allow yourself to regularly succeed. This is important, as if you do not feel successful, what motivation is there?

Several studies show that workers who are aware of the amount of work still to be completed and how close they are to achieving their goals are more motivated than workers who are just producing without any knowledge of the targets or quantity left to be produced. Target's people can visualize and achieve allow them to judge how much energy to conserve or spend. Anyone running a long distance athletic event knows the importance of judging the runner's time against the distance run. As the mile markers come up, you calculate your time from the start, your time for the last mile and how long it will take you to complete. This information boosts your performance. The same applies to completing goals within the build project. You know your schedule of works and what you have achieved, plus what pace you need to maintain to meet the completion date.

The 'How Longs'.

By listing these targets on a weekly time schedule, you can start to gage important points.

- How long before you have the first opportunity to commence?
- How long have you scheduled for identified items of work?

- How long do you consider the whole project will take to complete once started?

Each item has an individual time allocated to it. If your time schedule is set out in whole weeks, then follow this format.

The work schedule will be based on a standard eight-hour day and done by a 'normal' sized workforce. It's more likely you will have two bricklayers for six weeks than six bricklayers for two weeks.

Multiple tasks can take place during the same time period. In fact, the aim of the owner-builder is to have more than one trade working on-site at the same time. As two trades cannot share a restricted workspace, it is the manager's job to organize works at multiple places on a single house on the same day.

Consider how works will be tackled. For example, concrete can be mixed by a single mechanical mixer or can it be sped up by having two mixers both working at once. Perhaps for a larger pour it makes sense to organize ready-mix concrete deliveries by truck and to hire a concrete pump to deliver it to the right spot.

All three 'how long' options have time and cost implications. This self-discussion is the very point of the schedule of works.

What Types of Planning?

Stage Planning. Relating to a section of works. This could be focussed to a very detailed level on a certain trade or location. This could be, say, bathroom finishes and how the various trades cross over.

Weekly Planning. What you want to achieve each week in detail. It sets the challenge and relates back to the larger schedule.

Daily Planning. Set out verbally to the workers on site what you want to achieve each day and try again the next day and so on.

Compare the schedule of works to the list of costings to make sure all relevant points are included. You can refine both documents to provide calculated estimates of construction cost and work completion.

Getting Your Ducks in a Row.

A second schedule of works is also useful. This will be a schedule of the time you plan to take before commencing works on site. This pre-works schedule recognizes all the steps needed to meet both personal and regulatory issues. It takes time to 'get your ducks in a row'.

In Book 1, it was recommended you read building and style magazines, go to trade shows on building and take down great ideas from these, look at websites and tutorials for builders, and generally be an observational spy on all things building. With a journal, brochures and ideas in hand, you'll have a better idea of what you (and partner) really prefer and the program process will narrow that further.

After this, there are all the land purchase issues, as well as lending and budgeting points.

All in all, this project may well take as long to plan as it does to build. This sounds excessive, but believe me, good preparation is a must.

Critical Path.

What items are on your critical path? This is the path picking up which items must be ordered or complete before other items can commence. This also shows items not time critical in the first instance but which need to be completed in a timely manner. This indicates which items must be focused on and delivered on time to maintain progress.

Delegation.

The owner-builder is *not* expected to physically carry out each and every task on their own without guidance and assistance. If you are not a good accountant who is familiar with filing tax statements and Profit & Loss statements, then find someone who is. If you are not a skilled carpenter, employ someone to hang the doors. The build can be about you doing things you have never done before and it is also about acting smartly and effectively. Avail yourself of advice from others with expertise, intelligence and clear thinking.

What can be guaranteed is the unexpected. People will let you down at the last minute and state/province regulations and public bodies' rules, procedures and response times will appear to be designed by a sadist who is personally taking great pleasure in disrupting your build.

> **TIP BOX**
>
> *Don't Aim at Aspirations*
>
> A manager who is not in command of his subject can find site schedules difficult.
>
> If you do not feel you have the overall picture…
>
> If you are not aware of the schedule and how the different trades work together…
>
> If you do not know accurately what your financial position is…
>
> If you do not have defined goals…
>
> Then owner-building is a long and difficult process.

SMART Goals

To be successful, it is easier if you have points to aim for – i.e. goals.

Goals should be realistic, achievable, clear, measurable and act as targets. Without a target, you are moving towards an aspiration and it's a lot harder to achieve woolly aspirations than targeted goals.

SMART Goals are based on factors that focus on how things work. The SMART acronym stands for:

- S   Simple
- M   Measurable
- A   Attainable
- R   Relevant
- T   Time Based

By adopting the SMART approach, you break down the elements of your plan into achievable, bite size chunks. If you have not covered all of the components, ask yourself why this is.

Project Drivers.

The five main drivers of the project are:

Cost, Time, Quality, Risk & Safety.

In a perfect world, all these 'drivers' exist in harmony. The works are progressing to schedule, to a safe and high standard, with low risk and reasonable costs. Yet, none of the points exist in isolation. If you need to speed things up, will this risk a cost increase and reduce the quality of the works? If you need higher quality, will this slow progress down, incur greater overheads and cause extra costs through delays? If you need to cut costs, will this impact on the quality of product that can be purchased? Will this austerity mean safety is compromised and risk increased?

It is not impossible to have Cost, Time, Quality, Risk and Safety in balance, but it does take planning and delivery. This is where you get to develop the strategy and deliver on the tactics.

> **TIP BOX**
>
> **Keep Your Stress Levels Down**
>
> Mental health professionals are exploring mental health concerns within the construction industry. Recent figures produced by the Office for National Statistics (ONS) found men in the construction industry are three times more likely to take their own lives than men on average. (CIOB)
>
> The US National Institute for Occupational Safety and Health (NIOSH) study follows a 2019 report by *Drug and Alcohol Dependence*, which found that "construction workers are the most likely of all occupations to use cocaine and to take prescription opioids for non-medical purposes".
>
> Building and managing a build can be stressful. Be aware of the risks and strains involved in the process.
>
> The five top causes of work related stress are:
>
> - Too much work to do in the available time.
> - Travelling or commuting.
> - Responsibility for the safety of others.
> - Working long hours.
> - A dangerous job.

> Owner-Builders often check all these boxes. Stress is a major challenge; too much stress causes falls in productivity and increases the likelihood of poor decisions. This impacts on the quality of work and the quality of finish. This appears to be a worldwide issue.
>
> If someone you trust approaches you and raises concerns over your wellbeing, listen carefully.

Cost.

Cost is a crucial aspect comprehensively dealt with in our Money chapter in The Builder's Companion Book 1.

As project manager of your owner-build, you must allocate money and control spending. This is done through estimates you prepare and quotations you receive. The estimates are just that: your best guess. Quotations are offers from suppliers and contractors that can take different forms. These need to be scheduled neatly and checked and re-checked regularly. When issuing change orders to trades you should always ask three standard questions:

- Will it cost more?
- How much more?
- How long will it delay the schedule?

As works proceed, these will be updated and amended to ensure the following:

- You can afford to meet your expenses as they arise.
- You can complete the project, with sufficient funds in hand.
- You increase the value of the asset over and above your expenses, allowing you to re-mortgage the property with a regular mortgage on completion.
- You must reduce things that are high opportunities for stress.

Time.

Time is the only thing you can never recover or can be returned to you. Working in a timely manner is both an economic and a health issue.

It is economic because time on a construction project literally costs money. An example of this is an operative sweeping up and keeping the site safe and tidy.

This will continue for the length of time the project works are on site. If you're on site for 40 weeks instead of 20 weeks, the wage bill will be double. This simple example is replicated many times over. So allocate a time slot for each operation or trade and carefully monitor.

It is a health issue, as when works are behind schedule, matters become tense. A common scenario in which this vicious cycle plays out would be as follows. You are aware you have to complete certain works in order to claim money as part of your next application to your lender. You need this money to make a pro-forma payment to a supplier of an item scheduled for delivery. Another contractor is unhappy because he cannot start his work as the works in that area are not ready and the contractor who is delaying does not think he is in any way at fault. He blames the delay on external issues as the reason he cannot progress swiftly enough.

This situation is usually shortly followed by increased costs and a drop in quality. As you can imagine, this all leads to stress and can take a mental and physical toll on you.

Quality.

Quality is a mixture of standards and codes set by the state or province and enforced by the building inspection regime. They can be set by drawings, specifications, checklists and tests leading to the issue of certificates.

Quality is also the standards of the operatives' work and how well the component parts of his work fit together. Works completed properly to a high standard are a joy to look at. However, if a tile joint is off-center or a floor has undulations or if window openings do not line up, they will actually be acceptable from a building code perspective. But are they acceptable from your sense of quality of build?

Quality is also determined by the *style and feel* of a superior fitting. The most basic fitting will be cheaper to purchase and will functionally do the job, but it may never give the feeling of quality. This is not to say price is the only deciding factor, as sometimes the more basic component will do a good job and not be noticed. This is all about balance. The owner-builder must be vigilant and remember the aim is to have a high-quality home in every way. You do not want to end up with something with deficiencies you will be reminded of every time you walk through your home.

Risk.

Building works are risky, so how do you reduce or mitigate your risk?

As with all matters for the owner-builder, you have to be aware of an issue before you can deal with it. There are many things occurring all the time, even 'acts of God' which, simply put, are unusual occurrences outside of your control. You did not predict these to happen but they did happen. Although difficult to foresee, you can insure against some issues as a protective measure.

What problems can you reasonably foresee... things you can work out a way to reduce the impact of if they occur?

Retain Risk Yourself.

This seems counterintuitive, as we all wish to shed or at least spread risk.

You know the whole owner-builder business is inherently risky. You must purchase land, achieve planning permission and deliver a complicated build. That said, if you have confidence in your team and your consultants and you believe you can deliver the objectives you set, why not take the risk? Take responsibility and embrace the risk. Move forward, adopting tactics in the avoidance/risk transfer section.

Avoid Risk.

You can choose to buy a more expensive and less challenging product. You can elect not to push the design envelope and instead build a standard home with standard solutions. You can, alternatively, choose a greater level of consultant design and advice, including getting them to approve and confirm works are to a high quality and code compliant. This will increase the fees portion of the costs and thus reduce amounts which can be spent elsewhere.

Risk Transfer.

Consider which elements you are to carry out yourself and which elements you will instruct contractors to undertake. You may not feel confident you can successfully tackle certain jobs and complete them to a good standard. A risk transfer would be to employ a contractor to do this element of work. If serious defects become apparent, the trustworthy contractor will return and repair the problem.

This approach, guided by local laws, can be taken across the trades that do not have to be carried out by qualified specialist contractors. In the case of the specialist contractors, you can be comforted by experience and evidence of their insurances.

In some regions, it is a legal requirement for you to take out defect insurance on the whole project. Even if it is not a requirement, it is good practice to do so. The cost of the insurance and the responsibility remains with you. If you sell your property during the period of cover, the new owners can look to the insurance company. This does not reduce your risk in liability terms, but it allows a sale to occur which would not otherwise happen, your purchaser would probably be legally advised not to take the risk!

What are the common risks faced by the owner-builder and what can be done to mitigate matters?

Weather.

Weather changing season-to-season and day-to-day is not a surprise. Over the period of the construction works, you'll likely have many inclement days making works unproductive. Consider the location of your site and try to build the external works at what is thought the best building time of the year. An allowance in the schedule can be made for unproductive days.

Scope Creep.

This is when the works expand and additional areas or works are added to the project. Variations are considered which you feel will improve the overall quality of the home. If this is the case, carefully consider the implications.

- Do you need to revert to the planners and seek further permit approvals?
- Do you require further design input from the design team?
- Will this increase the projected costs?
- Will this delay the scheduled completion?
- Are the extra products/materials readily available?
- Will you require different contractors or more contractors?
- Will this increase your overheads and ongoing costs?

Scope Creep can best be avoided at the building permit stage, when your designs were frozen. The freezing took place so you could give accurate information to contractors and you could establish a budget. Scope expansion puts all that at risk.

Planners are aware of the tactics sometimes marshalled against them by applicants who believe they can get an improved building permit in phases. This is over and above what would have been granted in a single application. Naturally, they are becoming resistant to improving applications at a second bite. You and your team should carefully consider your permit application first-time.

Reduction Creep.

The opposite of scope creep is also a risk: *reduction creep*. This is the situation where you promised something within the permit application that in retrospect you would rather not do. Perhaps you were not aware of the strain the budget would come under until after approval was granted. This is not about improving or changing the layouts it's about omitting a feature that found favor during the application process.

After you have been granted the big picture, because of these constraints, you return to the planners to reduce your design. If this is anything to do with energy saving or carbon reduction, you are going to be increasingly fighting an uphill battle as improving the general environment is recognized as desirable. In fact, when they get used to your offer, they may find it hard to agree to you reducing anything at all. If they specifically listed items in the conditions which you propose to omit, their agreement could well be *unlikely*. Your team can advise you on these matters. Clarity over costs will reduce risk.

Incomplete Drawings and Specifications.

Like scope creep, this situation should not occur if you were diligent when the plans were frozen. I say 'you' because you are the owner, and the owner is ultimately responsible for all costs and delays. You must be sure of the design at the point it is frozen or else confusion will reign. If you are not sure, do not move ahead.

Carefully consider the areas under revision and be aware of the issues outstanding. Sometimes a situation occurs where the early part of the works are fast-tracked and instructed while later operations are still at the design stage. The risk is, the whole project is not yet decided on and costs can easily escalate before completion.

Slow Review Process.

You want most matters reviewed by your consultants in order to attain proper advice. In other cases, you'll want to amend their designs in order for your house to be covered by their insurance at a later time. You must keep up with the whole team of consultants and ensure they speedily respond so that progress and planning can continue to meet the time schedule.

Non-Compliance to Codes and Urban Myths.

This can be a tricky one. Many tradespeople feel sorry for their competition as they consider that not many of their rivals are as skilled as they are. This smugness and self-importance can be misplaced; sometimes they rely on their past knowledge of the rules as opposed to their reading of the rules. Things get amended and upgraded regularly and it can be a full-time job keeping up. I have heard on many occasions that something must be installed or positioned in a certain place or in a certain way because of mystical regulations or codes.

If you or particularly your building inspector thinks something is possibly amiss, simply ask for the name and reference of the regulation or code. Look it up (often easily available and free online) and see what it says for yourself. This more commonly occurs in peripheral and crossover matters rather than, say, in engineering, where the engineer will specify exactly how he wants structural works carried out.

Matters of interpretation that get caught up in this phantom non-compliance (urban myth) discussion are, for example:

- Distances from one fitting or outlet to another
- Gradient falls for drains and gutters
- Positioning of electrical points or isolators near wet areas
- Heights of balcony rails adjacent to a drop off the side

It is not that the contractor is trying to take advantage. They believe they are safeguarding you, but at the same time they do not always get all the current codes right. Often, they misunderstand the difference between what is required and how they like to do things.

> ### TRUE STORY
>
> I attended site one day with an electrical inspector. He asked the electrician why he had positioned the extract fan isolator outside of the bathroom. He was told that it was because of 'the codes'. The electrician could not be specific as to which particular regulation but he only positioned it there to comply. The inspector handed him a full codes book and as we were on the way out for a morning break, he invited the electrician to join us and even offered to buy him a hearty breakfast - if he could show us the code. We went on, but the electrician never appeared... it seems this regulation was an Urban Myth and did not exist.

A more serious issue is where an inappropriate or non-approved fitting is installed and it genuinely does not comply. Some areas have a requirement for a specific quality of products to be used. They must be marked with a government approved stamp, verifying the fitting is code compliant. Not all contractors believe this is important and may supply inferior products which are not compliant. There are ways of reducing this risk.

- Specify in your bid documents that only code compliant products are to be installed.
- Specify, as well as you can, what products are to be used. Refer to meeting a standard or code and also specifically list a certain manufacturer's product, if desired.
- Spot check items installed by services contractors, as this is the area of greatest code compliant product issues.
- Inform all contractors to specifically seek approval if they wish to use a product other than that specified.

Repairs to Works Improperly Carried Out.

This is perhaps the most heartbreaking for the supervisor. Something has been done wrongly and it is simply not good enough. Repairing it often causes as much grief as the original job. Obviously, if it is your employee, you take responsibility. If it's your contractor, you must take them to task. But ask yourself how it occurred. Were the works specified correctly? Did you verbally instruct something without specific design information? Were the works supervised correctly? Was it just that the operative knew no better and should have been guided or trained?

To reduce this risk, you must keep talking to the site operatives and impress on them the importance of high standards. Make sure they know what is expected of them.

Research by the Navigant Construction Forum found that across construction sites all over the globe a staggering 9-percent of site money spent was to put things right that had been incorrectly installed. The situation had occurred either due to miscommunication or poor workmanship.

This type of figure can make a massive difference to your budget. If saved, it matches the amount often proposed as a reasonable contingency.

Supplier Delays.

Specialized manufacturers are reluctant to manufacture any goods until they are signed off by the client's representative. Yet they cannot be signed off until working drawings have been created, circulated, commented upon and redrawn for each and every revision. This system is in place to reduce their risk.

The options are:

- Buy into their system
- Choose a different manufacturer

It can be painful working with careful suppliers as they do not appreciate your time issues or commitments. And they never will. They often have extended delivery periods or offer vague (within a certain week or month) delivery schedules.

The good side of the careful supplier is you are clear on what you will receive. The worry is, you just do not know when.

A look at high-quality owner-builder TV shows are almost unanimous in blaming the 'special' windows or doors supply as the point of delay. To reduce this type of risk, you need to specify the product early on and keep in contact with their whole team.

Regional Shortages.

From time to time, a manufacturing disaster or national/international emergency makes a product or material hard to acquire. I have over the years suffered through many shortages, including sheet material, bricks, cement and copper.

With the advent of manufactured goods coming from distant parts of the world, this is a situation which will not readily improve. There is no easy way out, so look for alternative products to meet your specified or planning requirements. A friendly relationship with your local builders' hardware stores never goes amiss and sometimes it is important *who* you know…

The Covid-19 pandemic has caused material shortages and manufacturing delays. Many companies around the world reduced production levels or cannot deliver some products to certain markets. You can only react to issues as they arise but remember you have to keep communicating with suppliers and remain focused on a smooth delivery schedule for your site as part of the reality of constant management negotiations.

Contractor Default.

This one can come out of the blue. Often a contractor fails because of issues that are nothing to do with you or your works but you are affected. To defray this risk, you can try to screen contractors and see if they seem stable. Watch out for 'red flags' as discussed in 'Good Deal' in Chapter 12, but be aware, even large corporations and governments get caught out from time to time.

To protect yourself, you must not pay for materials upfront or off-site. For works not complete, pay carefully. You are in a much stronger position if you are holding money on a contractor.

Theft.

Security is an issue and you must be careful both when the site is operational and when it is closed. Plan site security and have fencing at the boundaries and a secure lock-up in place. Be more security conscious towards the end of the project, as this is when thieves know more valuable goods will be fitted. The risks are delays and expenses from replacing lost goods and repairing damage occurring when the stolen goods were forcibly removed.

Damage and Vandalism.

Damage is a stressor far beyond your cost and inconvenience. It is often carried out by juveniles who do not appreciate how dangerous construction sites can be. If they hurt themselves, then all sorts of questions can be raised over your negligence in allowing them to enter. To confirm, this means entering without your permission. Signage is not sufficient as you cannot be sure the intruder can read. You must demonstrate you have taken sufficient care to reduce the risk to reasonably stop people entering without permission.

Offsite Production, aka Modern Methods of Construction (MMC).

Risks can be transferred by off-site production. This means having products delivered and fitted that were put together in a manufactured kit form. It can consist of pre-cast floor panels with insulation factory-fitted and glued, or a pod arriving on site already kitted out. Manufacturers can give assurances of cost and delivery and they can be at work off-site while you are at work on earlier scheduled construction items.

A cost engineer (CE) can help you devise a budget and advise on financial risk. Their role is to steer you away from overspends on your budget.

The above measures mitigate risk but will not eliminate it. As an owner-builder, a level of risk is always with you, but by planning, you can share a portion of this risk with others.

The owner-builder may be the master of his own ship, but he is not always the master of his own destiny. He can plan and pronounce on matters and sometimes he will not win but usually he will. The whole of the project must be guarded. By always doing things deliberately, you should ensure the losses will never come to anything as large as the wins.

Chapter 2 – Action

- Monitor/Plan, Monitor/Plan, Monitor/Plan
- You carry all the responsibility: get your first aid kit; ensure security
- Consider SMART Goals
- Specify exact products and compliance codes
- Develop a Schedule of Works
- Identify the critical path

CHAPTER 3
SUMMARY

You set the standards for your site safety. There are national standards of course, but the buck stops with the owner-builder.

Highlights covered in this chapter include:

- Self-preservation is important, as well as protecting others
- Enforce OH&S across the site – do not drop standards
- Leadership is required

CHAPTER 3

HEALTH & SAFETY

'The A, B, C of it will save you if you follow it: Always Be Careful'.
— Colorado School of Mines Magazine

Occupational Health & Safety (OH&S) on site is important to you. It may well be the subject everyone wants to avoid since it does not push the project forward when all is going well, but it can really put you back if something goes wrong. Even if you ignore OH&S, it will not ignore you. It will sneak up and provide more stress than you want to imagine.

But surely the workers on site are professionals who are used to working in the construction site environment and know how to look after themselves.

This internal statement is, sadly, not true. Sometimes accidents are so dumb that you wonder why they occurred. When looking back on what occurred, it is sometimes almost inconceivable that an accident could have happened in any way other than the recklessness of certain individuals.

Well, you might think, if people choose to be reckless, what can you do about it?

Legally, you have to do lots about it. It is the owner-builder's responsibility to make sure the site is safe, as it is a workplace. You do this by insisting that the site is well run and risks are reduced.

This takes imagination, planning and determination.

Safety by Walking Around.

An accident is by definition an unplanned occurrence, and it is your responsibility to reduce the opportunities of unplanned occurrences. Whenever you are walking around the site, keep your eyes open and be aware of safety issues. However, you do not need to plan safety checks; they are part of the ongoing daily routine.

Accidents often occur because the operative has a misguided belief that he is helping to get the job done. Rather than wait for more equipment or take the time to safely access an area, he does something that is recognized as dangerous to onlookers. Yet he is confident he can achieve the task and that the risk is manageable.

The other cause of accidents is the owner-builder not providing safety equipment as part of their site set up. For example, you ask an operative to access an area by ladder, but a mobile tower was appropriate. A different version of this is contractor resource. You must ask each contractor if they have sufficient safety equipment and safety strategies in place. If an accident occurs and the contractor claims that they could not afford the proper equipment as you had not allowed sufficient funding within their priced works, they may be able to join you into a safety claim. As owner-builder you are connected to everything. As part of your instruction to contractors you should check they intend to carry out all operations in a safe way.

Remember, if it all goes horribly wrong, all injured parties will be looking to you for compensation.

TRUE STORY

> A builder I know had an unexpected visit from a safety inspector. A neighbour may have alerted them to the site or they may have visited just because they decided to. All went well until the inspector noticed a defective ladder that was owned by a plumbing contractor and had only arrived on site that day. Although the builder did not own the ladder or was even aware of its existence he was fined. The responsibility lies with the owner-builder who must be vigilant and not allow unsafe plant or unsafe occurrences.

It's only an accident *after* things go wrong. Before that, it is a near miss. You can learn from a near miss. So, if you see something happening on site that could be dangerous, stop that activity and ensure that it is carried out in a safer manner.

This can be something simple, like a missing handrail, which could lead to a fall from a height, or a board covering a hole in the floor that is not strong enough to take the load of an overweight builder. By reacting to what you can see, you set the attitude for a safe approach to the works.

Q. If nothing goes wrong, what does it matter?

Be aware that you can face substantial fines for allowing poor practices to operate, even if there is no injury as a result. The responsibility for safe working is everyone's and the penalty can also be widely shared.

Q. Who is responsible?

The owner-builder/project manager is at the front of the queue and is either solely responsible or has shared responsibility for nearly everything.

Designers must ensure, as far as they can through their designs, that the building as designed does not pose a OH&S risk to the constructors or future occupants.

Workers must take reasonable care for their own OH&S and that of their fellow workers. They must comply with reasonable instructions and safeguards to maintain or improve site safety. This stipulation does not lift full responsibility from the owner-builder.

Occupational Health & Safety On Site - Familiarity Breeds Contempt.

Contractors are professionals familiar with site conditions and operate on a building site on a daily basis, however, the theory that 'familiarity breeds contempt' as far as OH&S is concerned is plausible. Many contractors carry out 'tool box talks' which are site-based OH&S discussions and 'read' written safety notices and instruction sheets until they are almost oblivious to the message.

To combat this, there has been a recent move by building site managers to provide files of paperwork and erect signs instructing operatives to act safely at all times. They operate in the belief that because they can prove they have, in writing, informed the worker to act safely, their responsibility in the case of an accident is reduced.

This is not the case. The person in charge of the site will be forced by law to take responsibility.

At the most basic level of self-preservation in a legal and financial sense, an accident can be deemed or become *more* your fault. But this responsibility can be reduced, and risks shared, if you take a few simple steps to keep people safe and effectively warn people of dangers.

Who do you keep safe?

Everyone.

Everyone includes site visitors, consultant professionals, workers, members of the general public or unauthorized intruders. A duty can be placed on clients, principal contractors, principal designers and contractors to share and use health and safety information.

In all likelihood, if an accident happens, you will not be discussing this with the victim but rather their legal representatives. These lawyers will be astounded by the most minor contravention of the strictest OH&S regimes and seek compensation from you.

Leadership.

Leadership is an important aspect of management. How you lead affects how people react. From an OH&S perspective, you must lead by having a safe site. You may try to be authoritative or democratic, chief coach or coercive leader; the style will follow your personality. The important point is: you must be firm on safety.

Safety is not a choice. You have a legal duty to have a safe site. This requirement is regardless of cost and convenience. The duty must be complied with if it is possible within the current state of knowledge and technology.

Where there is blame, there is a claim!

It is up to you as owner-builder to set the standard. OH&S must not be allowed to evolve. It is ultimately the client's responsibility to ensure any and all contractors have sufficient resources to maintain high levels of OH&S. If the senior people who you employ as contractors are sloppy about their own OH&S and their workforce, what are they like with other aspects of their work?

It is good practice for written OH&S documents to be produced before any works commence and each contractor should produce additional documentation as their operations come into play.

It is also good practice to have information about emergency services and the address of the local Accident and Emergency Department posted in a prominent position. This is to reduce delays in finding out where to seek help in an emergency. Professionals are available to prepare documentation and advise on OH&S.

There is a lot of information available on OH&S in the construction industry and it is worthwhile familiarising yourself with your obligations and the responsibilities of others.

The basic starting point is: all workers and all members of the public must be safe. Safe means they are not subject to long term health risks such as by exposure to dangerous materials or to risk of personal injury. How you ensure safety in an inherently dangerous situation is the point of the whole exercise.

Safety Begins with You.

Safety begins in your selection of contractor and their attitudes. Money is not saved by untidy or dangerous working; in fact, untidy sites promote waste and damage.

All contractors or others providing services must be adequately insured. It is good practice to ask for evidence of all insurances applicable from anyone providing a service.

If you are acting as principal contractor, with no-one else in charge, then you have to *act* as principal contractor. A competent principal contractor would has signage on site, informing anyone who comes onto your site of the basic OH&S rules of the workplace. These signs can be purchased inexpensively and they set the tone for what is expected.

All equipment should be in good order and fit for purpose. The principal contractor usually provides extension cords and power points around the site for the tradespeople to utilize. Battery-run tools have improved to the point of becoming mainstream because they have become so much more efficient. They can produce great results without the need for trailing cords and therefore the possibility of electrocution.

All machine operators must be suitably qualified and all machines must be in good order. Never be afraid to ask machine hire companies for evidence of compliance and competence.

Basic safety equipment and personal protective equipment (PPE) should be available to all operatives, provided by either you as owner-builder or by the contractor/tradespeople. These include: high visibility clothing, hard hats, goggles, gloves and boots.

Access to heights off the floor should only be via safe working platforms or scaffolds and should be competently erected and maintained. Regular inspection is mandated.

Consider All Operations.

All site operations should be individually considered. On larger, professional sites, the compliance regime often requires a written risk assessment for each operation. This will be time-consuming, but it does ensure OH&S considerations are forefront and safety procedures are followed. A decision must be taken as to the appropriate level of formalized OH&S and how much informal OH&S is allowed on site.

It should not be your only concern, but if an incident occurs and anyone at all is injured, then your liability can be very far-reaching. It is imperative *insurance* is in place if an operative or member of the public is injured; you cannot rely on others being responsible for their own insurance. By all means, insist all contractors have insurance and let the discussions take place after an accident between insurance companies over liability and responsibility.

Facilities.

On-site worker facilities are also the responsibility of the principal contractor. The level of on-site facilities should be commensurate with the scale of operation, but basic hand washing, toilet, and power availability are now pretty much universal. You should also have a First Aid kit on site. Again, facility requirements vary in different locations. An example of this is some areas require hot running water be available for the operatives' use during construction, while others allow basic cold running water. It is up to the site management or controller to determine what the requirement is and apply the appropriate rules as a minimum. In warmer climates, site refrigerators are the norm. Find out what is expected and reasonable.

Fire.

As everyone knows, fire can destroy buildings and kill people. This terrifying scenario can take place while buildings are under construction or after they are complete.

Fire is commonly cited as needing three things to survive, which are known as the 'triangle of fire'.

- Fuel – organic material is needed to feed the fire
- Oxygen – air is needed to sustain flames and the combustion process
- Heat – different materials have different heat levels to reach the point of combustion

If you could construct your building so that it omits at least one of the three triangle points, no building would suffer from a fire out of control. This has only been achieved in the most controlled conditions, and as far as I am aware, never in a domestic situation. So, you are always going to be in danger of your property burning down, with the added potential to suffer loss of life. But knowledge of the basics of fire generation will assist you in avoiding the circumstances where fire will thrive.

There is a fourth element 'chemical reaction' so it is actually a 'tetrahedron' (a triangular pyramid) rather than a triangle but this is not nearly as memorable but as before, by taking one of the four elements away fire will be extinguished.

Fire Tetrahedron

Poor assessment and lack of vigilance is the clear link between building operations and fires occurring on site.

What Can You Do?

During the works, take sensible precautions and assess the fire risk of every operation. Obviously, any operation with sparks or open flame are operations to pay particular attention to. Other less obvious risks occur, for example, where glass is left in the open sunshine. This can magnify heat onto paper or cardboard, etc. Also, after an operation is over and all tools put away, this is still a time of heightened risk for hot works completed earlier. Latent combustion can occur.

After works are complete and the property is occupied, there is still a risk of fire and consequent injuries and death. Not a nice thought, but you have the power to meet this challenge.

Construct the building strictly in line with the building codes. If you do this, your property will be very safe.

The building inspector is not a site supervisor but an assessor. He assesses what he sees and what he believes. If you 'pull the wool over his eyes' and do not faithfully carry out the works properly, then your whole build is at risk. This is especially the case with fire protection matters. Too often, fire spreads because of installation problems, not because of design problems.

Automatic Fire Suppression Systems (AFSS).

Many construction professional bodies believe that AFSS water-based sprinkler systems are cost effective and reduce the damage caused by fire. International insurance giant, Zurich Municipal, has carried out research and state that: "Sprinklers don't only save lives, buildings and water they save money too".

It is commonly believed that water suppression causes more damage than the fire. This has been found not to be the case. By installing an automatic system, the sprinkler heads are activated individually and only the ones directly over the fire are operational. A sprinkler head will spray 15 US gallons (60 liters) of water a minute compared to a firefighter's hose which will produce 160 US gallons (600 liters) a minute. Less water equals less damage and less drying out.

Risk Management.

The owner-builder must identify possible hazards that arise because of the works. These are situations that may occur but also may not, so you need to use imagination to review how things may work out. Lots of information is available on managing OH&S on building sites, and a review of some publications and articles will help you realise what may happen.

The type of hazards commonly encountered are:

- Hidden live services, which are uncovered underground or within walls, floors, etc.
- Falls from height
- Falling objects
- Inappropriately placed materials
- Hazardous materials
- Dust and particles in the atmosphere
- Fragile roofs
- Vibration and hazardous noise

This list is only a small review of what may be included in a hazard assessment.

Assess the hazards and then determine the measures to be introduced to control the risk:

- Identify which operations are at risk
- Which parts of the work are causing the risk?
- Which control measures are you recommending?
- Review existing control measures

Control Measures.

Once an item of work has been identified as a risk, the most effective control is to eliminate it from the works. An example of this would be battering the sides of an excavation as opposed to having vertical earth. By eliminating the vertical wall, you have greatly reduced the risk. This control measure would not cause great expense either but would be very effective.

If you are unable to substitute works or eliminate works completely, then it is your responsibility to reduce the remaining risk. To follow on with the excavation example, the trench should be securely shored to support the sides to meet the engineer's design. This keeps people safe when working in an exposed area. The safety and maintenance of the trench could also be improved by a sump dug into the base and a water pump available to dewater the base.

Safe Working Method Statement (SWMS).

A good way of understanding the risks and communicating the risks is by preparing a SWMS. In most municipal areas, owner-builders are not required by law to produce written documents, but if you do produce written information and procedures this does show intent. A SWMS evidences your wish for a safety-first approach at any later tribunal or investigation.

You should include all the elements, such as labor, plant and material, and conclude how the works are controlled. This gives you a starting point when you are instructing operatives who will actually carry out the works. You will not be relieved of responsibility, but the level of responsibility may be reduced. All matters should be subject to ongoing review. It is good to ask contractors which safety provisions they are including. After all, they may have documents they can share with you that allow you to monitor safety as their works proceed. Your state or province may well provide information and fact sheets on OH&S subjects. If not why not check out neighboring states/provinces online information?

To ensure that the highest standards are maintained, consultation and reviews of OH&S should be ongoing and regular. If the OH&S or SWMS are found not to be 100 percent effective, then update and revise them to the best of your ability. Again, professionals can be called on for advice.

Site Set Up.

The works on a construction site progress every working day and so hazards can spring up daily. Planning from the beginning and maintaining a safe site is the best way to minimise accidents and increase productivity.

Contamination.

Consider the previous use of the land and check historical documents. Was the land contaminated? Or perhaps the building had basements that were used to store commercial products or hazardous substances?

Asbestos.

Was an asbestos survey carried out to identify areas that need isolation or protection? Any demolition must be planned in a way that complies with OH&S regulations on asbestos. Your design team can assist with advice on compliance.

Electricity.

To progress building works, you can obtain a temporary builder's electricity supply. This will be taken from the main supply to a convenient single point on your site by your electrician. All extension cords on site should be Heavy-Duty and be rated to draw up to 15 amps of power.

Electricity can be a hidden killer. It cannot be smelt or heard, so even if dangerous, it may not be apparent until electrocution happens. Because of this, the site power system should only be installed and maintained by a qualified electrician. If a breaker regularly trips, the electrician should investigate the reasons. Battery-powered tools should be used whenever possible.

Extension Cords.

Simple rules to make electrically powered extension cords safe(r);

- Be careful where they are running - especially through doorways
- Inspect them to check for damage
- Ensure the power source is fused so that they will stop working in a fault condition
- Do not extend one cord with another
- Do not fix leads with nails or staples
- Do get them regularly tested

Working at Heights.

The largest cause of fatal accidents and injuries is falling from heights. Many are falls of less than 6' 6"(2m.); Many accidents occur because workers do not use ladders and scaffolds safely. It's sometimes tempting to save time and just get things done. If an accident occurs, the full weight of the law will speedily come down, and the consequences for you as manager can be serious.

Scaffolds.

Scaffolds should only be erected by professionals. Ensure the workers are qualified with both theoretical and practical knowledge. Scaffolding should only be erected, altered and dismantled by workers who are trained and qualified or working under the direct supervision of someone who is. A scaffold must be safe and secure. Regular checks should be carried out and evidenced.

Digging.

Going down into the ground can be dangerous, so careful consideration is required before you excavate. Assume the presence of services when digging, even if none are indicated or shown on drawings. Check with all utility providers first and then use detection devices to check the locations of services ahead of excavation.

Service pipes and lines are placed at recommended depths, but never assume they are always installed where they should be. Services can appear similar, so always be careful to identify each service correctly. Only dig with insulated spades and shovels to safely uncover live services; over-excavation with power tools is a common cause of accidents.

What you can do is:

- Avoid working at height where possible
- Where work cannot be avoided at height, take safety measures and use the correct equipment
- Where you cannot eliminate the risk of a fall, take measures to minimise the distance of the fall
- Avoid working on fragile roofs
- Ensure ladders and scaffolds are properly maintained
- Scaffolds should be regularly inspected
- Assume every service is live until you can prove otherwise

Good Practice Check Box

Item	Good Practice	Check Yes
ABC	Always be careful	
Information	Written SWMS	
First Aid	Kit available at all times	
Insurance	Display. Obtain sub contractors' insurance	
Site Security	Site hoarding to secure boundaries	
PPE	High viz & hard hats	
Safety Information	Signage at entrance	
Water	Clean running water. Heated?	
Toilet Facilities	Portable washroom	
Lighting	To all work areas	
Power	Cables safely run to all areas	
Work at Height	Safety rails	
Ladders	Labelled for weight etc.	
Hazards	Stairs clear and clean to prevent trips	
Scaffold	Regular checks - alterations by authorized persons only	
Access Tower	Safety first	
Mechanical Equipment	Authorized operators only	
Tools & Equipment	Battery operated	

TRUE STORY

Horror Stories

In the past few years, there have been many horror stories.

1. A young policeman was returning home quite late at night from a bar and he stopped to talk to his friend. He leaned onto a building site fence for a little stability. He had not rushed at it, he had just leaned on it for support. The fence had not been left secure over the weekend and it collapsed. It collapsed inwards and he fell into a basement. He died as a result of the fall.

* * *

2. A builder had a delivery of windows quite late in the day. To get them out of the way, he stored them on a scaffold at first floor level. A young woman was passing by the next day and a strong wind gusted and lifted a window into the air. It landed on the young woman. She died as a result of her injuries.

* * *

3. A young Mom pushing a stroller was passing by a construction site while a delivery of bricks was underway. During off-loaded a pack of bricks separated, spilling a few bricks. A brick struck the young mother but spared the baby. The woman died as a result of her injuries.

These are not scare stories; they are actual occurrences and were all widely reported in the media. All were avoidable but all ended in tragedy.

After Completion.

After the building is occupied, maintenance continues throughout the life of the building. If any item of repair or maintenance disturbs the fire protection system, do not leave it incomplete. The fire protection is there for a reason.

Chapter 3 – Action

- Review OH&S
- What notifications must you make before commencing works?
- Check everyone's insurance before they commence on site
- Consider when you need SWMS (*Safe Working Method Statements*)
- Do safety checks by walking about

MONEY/TIME
Budget & Cash Flow
Finance Timings
Book Valuation With Lender's Surveyor
Update Work Program

DESIGN
Product Reviews
Seek Quotations

WORKS
Place Orders
Check On Green Credentials

CHAPTER 4
SUMMARY

Your destination is to construct a high standard home. You must chart your way to a high quality finish.

Highlights covered in this chapter include:

- What does completion mean?
- How do you manage boundaries?
- Quality Assurance and Quality Control
- Defects (Punch) list

CHAPTER 4

HOW TO FINISH

'From Soup to Nuts'.

– Unknown

'From soup to nuts' describes the courses of a meal from beginning to end. In this case, you want to calmly go through the whole cooking process and enjoy the finished product. Planning involves laying out the full menu and listing all the ingredients for the entire meal.

Similarly, with building, at every stage you have an eye on what will be required next and ultimately what is needed at the finish. The finale is to produce a fine home for your family to enjoy, constructed to meet your personal needs. If it is cheaper than you could have purchased an equivalent home for, so much the better.

How Do You 'Finish' Before You Have Started?

Simply, you start at the desired end – so, logically, you finish at the beginning! The only way to avoid having lots of defects and imperfections on completion is to pick them up as works proceed. It is unreasonable to imagine defects will never occur. It's how you deal with them that makes the difference. Be aware of the common mistake of thinking something is not important enough to get right. The small details do matter.

The time to raise issues over quality is while the supplier or contractor is on site, including issues about how two different contractors' works are seen when side by side. Poor work can simply be something not installed properly, either because of lack of skill or lack of pride in the quality of the finished product.

To combat this, there are codes of practice and specifications to ensure minimum standards are met. Sometimes, things just do not look right, even if technically they meet the codes. The other main cause of poor work is boundary issues, aka contractual interface. One tradesperson's standard of finish is affected by another's work. This is where the *management* comes into 'boundary management'.

The Primary Task of the owner-builder is to build the house. This is the big picture result all parties are working towards. As owner-builder, delivering the completed house and all this encompasses is your goal. Look into all matters falling within this remit and avoid all other points outside of this. You 'stick to your own knitting' and let others do their own thing.

> **TRUE STORY**
>
> Many years ago, I was acting as the principal contractor for a local government scheme upgrading a riverside pedestrian area. A specialist client-nominated contractor was to install distinct pineapple-shaped steel finials to a long fence. The contractor did not attend site as per the schedule and I enquired as to the reason for the delay. His excuse was 'the boy was on holiday' and he could not install the finials without assistance.
>
> To follow the 'stick to one's knitting' creed, I had to advise him to employ other available labor, as he was delaying the progress of works. It was his responsibility to provide sufficient and timely labor and so I did not get directly involved in helping him source labor or offer to provide labor. I like to offer assistance with something routine, like unloading or storage, but the actual operatives (the boy), the quality of work and other risks are entirely the contractor's concern.

The character of the construction industry is unique, with all operations occurring in a temporary workplace, populated by workers engaged by several different businesses mixed in with self-employed contractors. Materials are manufactured by innumerable companies around the globe and sold to you through agents, who all deliver separately. The whole process is fraught with weather concerns as you are building a structure in open air conditions across the seasons.

This set up has been described as 'independent autonomy'. You want the savings and efficiencies of specialist contractors who can be introduced to the works and depart when their section is complete, but this means you cannot directly control their comings and goings.

The owner-builder is tasked with arranging matters and leading people towards a common goal, yet understand they are subject to different pressures. Different trades working to different methods and time scales leads to uncertainty over exactly what will happen next. The owner-builder, acting as site manager, knows what he has scheduled to happen. But as they say, you don't always get what you want, when you want it. How you deal with this reality is what will determine the quality of the build.

As well as getting works ready to meet the site schedule, you need the next team of operatives arranged to be on site, with the correct materials sitting in planned positions. These materials must be in the right quantities, to the right quality and to the right price. If you are responsible for providing plant or access equipment, this too needs to be in place.

Boundary Management.

Boundary management is as stated 'managing boundaries'. Each trade has an expertise and works within their remit. Many operatives work on more than a single project at a time, so other works outside your control factor into what happens on *your* site.

As operatives are all working on a single project in the same site environment, it is understandable that their boundaries will cross over and occasionally clash. They are issued with both general specifications and task-specific information only relating to them. Examples of this occurring abound, but basically, they fall into the following main categories:-

Two People Work at the Same Point After the First is Complete.

This is the most common of all the cases. Everyone on site follows on from the concreter, who laid the concrete floor slab. The carpenter has to erect his timber walls on top of the slab. If the surface is not level, the carpenter can either run his walls not to level or spend time correcting his wall due to someone else's poor workmanship. The boundary to be managed is between the concreter and carpenter. The next boundary is between the carpenter and drywall installer and so on.

Two People Want to Work in the Same Space at the Same Time.

Two trades are both on site and both would like to work in the same zone. This requires management of the spaces and the manager should have been alerted to this by the site schedule of works. Both operations will be listed as ongoing at the same time. The first point to consider is if either trade is on the critical path. This means one operation has to be completed before other works may commence. Priority should be given to this contractor as it will affect others starting. But if both trades wish to work in the same area, the owner-builder must make the call and ask one contractor to move to a different zone or rearrange their time on site.

Two People are Needed to Make Something Work.

This situation can often occur in relation to services installation. Perhaps an electrician is set to supply a power point for another specialist installer. The circuit position must be agreed by both parties, otherwise it is likely to be in an unfavorable position. The electrician must have knowledge of the load the circuit will carry, or else how can he install the correct cable and fuse? The specialist installer must specify the type of connection he will be making, or otherwise how will the electrician supply the correct item? Is it hard-wired or plugged in?

All these situations need good boundary management between the two contractors for the installation works to progress smoothly.

More Than One Person Works on Something Provided by Someone Else.

An example of where this scenario can occur is the fitting of the kitchen base units. After the base units are fixed, a template needs to be taken for the stone worktop. Two further jobs remaining are the second fixing of the electrical wall power points and tiling the backsplash. All are important but you must decide the sequence of the work.

Quality Control

To keep on top of all the issues over work standards, you need to institute your own quality control procedures. This is more of an informal process because it first requires you to keep up with progress on all fronts and be aware of what is occurring. Tradespeople do not like being cross-examined over the quality of their work and finish but they are invariably pleased to see an interest in their works.

As part of your management role, discuss the finish offered and if this causes issues for follow-on trades. If you are instinctively not happy, but you cannot be sure *how* or *if* it should be tackled, then phone a friend to get a second opinion. This may be one of your consultants or a friend with expertise in the area of concern. A trouble shared often assists in allowing you to marshal your thoughts and work towards a solution.

Whenever a trade is close to completing their section or package, take the time to closely look at what is proffered as complete and see if it works. If it's a floor slab, check if it is level; if it's a window, does it open and close properly. The duty of the contractor is to offer you a good job. Nonetheless, the onus is on you to check because long after all the others are gone, you will be on your own facing the realities.

In addition, keep a paper (or electronic) trail of all site instructions and regularly capture images of on-site progress. General images can often be of real assistance as they capture all sorts of things in the background. It is helpful for images to be timed and dated. This creates a record of on-site conditions at a given point.

Raising Concerns.

First raise issues with the operatives on site who undertook the actual work. After this, it is a matter of escalation through the management structure and onwards. Almost always, matters are easily resolved on-site through positive discussion. But if necessary, put your concerns forward formally in writing. One of the purposes of an information trail is to clearly determine who is responsible for an item or quality of work.

If you have kept up your end of the bargain, providing information and materials in a timely manner as well as paying invoices promptly, then you are usually in a good bargaining position. If you are unclear if an item of work is acceptable or not, do not make the final payment until you are.

Keeping up-to-date on your finances is a crucial tool in finishing. Always look ahead and ask yourself if you can afford to meet contractors' invoices. Are sufficient funds available?

Budgets are prepared for the main items before commencement of the project. During works, sometimes items arise which were not explicitly allowed for or you were persuaded to increase the quality of an item or finish. If this has a financial effect, then you must consider the cost implications. If you cannot afford this cost now, it will affect your ability to finish. You must make a judgement call on the matter and issue a clear instruction.

This instruction may be not to complete this item now but rather return at a future time and complete it as you would prefer it done. Whatever the case, it is your responsibility to make an informed decision. If you decide to omit an item from current works, leave it tidy around this item. It will be clear something is missing but at least the surrounding works will be complete.

Defects List.

Punch List is the informal name for the list of defective or incomplete items noted after works were offered as complete. The list states items, that are still to be completed or require improvement. You are asking the contractor to complete defective or unfinished items.

	Contractor	Signed Off
Ground Floor		
Level Points Above Worktop	AKA Electrical	
Certificates - All	AKA Electrical	
Labels to CCU	AKA Electrical	
Confirm all Appliances Operational and Fixed	AKA Electrical	
Install Shelf Under Kitchen Sink	Carpenter	
Repair Shelf to Edge of Microwave	Carpenter	
Clean Stains Off Front Paved Area	Jim	
Clear Materials from Rear Garden	Jim	
Issue Gas Certification	Fast Gas	
• *Highlight the items applicable to a specific contractor.* • *Name a person /company/ trade.* • *Ask Contractor to return sheet indicating completion.*		

Discuss completion with each trade contractor and set them to work completing all the points listed. Ask them to let you know when their work is complete.

Then you re-check and if you are not happy, discuss this further and reissue an amended list. At the end you are crystallizing what needs to be done and if there are problems then you want to be able to deal with them.

The objective is not simply to come up with issues at the end; the objective is to get all the works properly completed.

Many IT apps are now available to list and record defective works. These tools are there to make your life easier and inform the appropriate person of the issues. Take advantage of these technologies and keep everyone informed.

Close to project completion, jointly list all the defects, starting from a logical point or room and methodically coming out to the external front area. If the list is long, divide it into groups or trades and issue the relevant information on 'their' items to suppliers and contractors. If the contractor returns the list indicating completion, this will be very helpful, but more likely, you will have to keep on top of the situation and keep a record of the state of play.

Encourage the contractors to finish off snags to one specific area at a time, as opposed to going all over the place. The best way to finish a house is one room at a time. Having a methodology creates a sense of achievement.

An important component of finishing is evidence of completion by certificates. These may be self-certified by the contractors or you may need independent verification. Whatever the situation, this is part of the completion process. Missing certificates are placed on the punch list with all other unfinished items.

When it comes to the whole project, the definition of 'finished' can be important. To meet planning permit requirements, you may need to have finished by a certain date. To attain a mortgage, you may need to demonstrate you are technically finished. The best way of proving your build is indeed finished is to have the building deemed habitable by the building inspector. Although, as you may find, even a certificate issued at this point can allow some items to remain unfinished. In some locations, painting is not considered as a requirement for the building to be habitable. So, find out what constitutes habitable and decide what you can consider as finished.

What are the Differences Between Quality Assurance (QA) and Quality Control (QC)?

QA and QC have many similarities but they are different.

QA is ensuring you install the item correctly first time. Be sure what standards and specification you want the item to meet and how you want it installed. Read up on manufacturers' literature and good practice guides. If in any doubt, issue a copy of the regulation or issue a sketch or write a description detailing how you want the job tackled.

QC is checking the job was installed correctly and verifying this through a test (visual) or through certification.

You have to complete QA before you can start QC.

This is not always easy, but if you have a process, it becomes standard practice. Talk to every contractor regularly and question if they have any quality issues. The more aware you are, the higher the standard of works produced.

What to Do?

Here's an imagined scenario of how you might end up agreeing to accept poor quality of works. In this instance, it's a person fixing drywall to a wall someone else built.

If the wall is not square to the adjacent walls, neither will the drywall be. Following on, neither will the baseboard fixed to the surface, nor will the piece of furniture placed against the wall. So, the issue is with the wall, not what followed on.

At the stage of the drywall board fixing, you have three options:

- Amend the wall
- Amend the drywall board
- Do nothing at all and live with it

Too often this goes unnoticed until the furniture moving in stage, and with carpets down, this all seems too hard to fix, hence you unknowingly accepted inferior work.

When works are complete, your only reasonable option is No.3 as the others are relatively expensive. The cost of correction is out of kilter with the benefits of the remedy. By acting when works are installed, you have the opportunity to get the works finished properly.

Only by your vigilance at each stage can this or similar situations be avoided.

Chapter 4 – Action

- Talk to everyone on site every day
- Keep records of instructions
- Take images around the build
- Compile certificates as you go
- Add items to punch lists

MONEY/TIME
Budget & Cash Flow
Finance Timings
Pay Contractors/Suppliers

DESIGN
QA & QC
Seek Quotations

WORKS
Manage Boundaries
Meet Contractors
Appoint Contractors
Infrastructure Orders

CHAPTER 5
SUMMARY

This is the start point. From here on in, you are in charge.

Highlights covered in this chapter include:

- Purchasing policy
- OH&S facilities
- Pick the right tools/equipment to do the job
- Set out the foundations
- Inspect works as soon as offered as complete
- Raise any issues at the earliest time you can

CHAPTER 5

START WORKS

'Unless there are clear lines of accountability, as in who is responsible for doing what, no-one is accountable'.

– Dr. Martin Parkinson

After all your preparations, you actually start work. This milestone can sneak up on you; the time difference between 'planning to start' and an actual start is often blurred. It is rare you actually commence works at a certain time on a certain date.

Sites are purchased in a variety of conditions; each one is individual but they are always challenging. They range from sites with structures scheduled for demolition, to vacant land never previously developed.

It is important that before you commence any works at all, you ensure you have fully conformed with all health and safety notifications and requirements. You must have adequate contractor's insurance in place too, and this may be at risk if your paperwork is not up to date and compliant. Accidents and subsequent claims can start at any point of the process. Lenders often dictate the level of insurance that must be taken out and wish to see evidence of it before they will advance any funds.

Works you commence today are based on yesterday's forecasts. Therefore, it is important you keep account of how site works progressed today, so you can update your forecasts for tomorrow. This sounds glib but it's true. Keep relating progress to your schedule of works and update it as necessary.

Getting Things Moving.

Getting what you need to site, when you need it, at the quality needed and for the right price to meet the schedule of works can be a real challenge. The owner-builder is responsible for doing everything needed to get things moving. This may seem a very broad description, and it is. Wherever you can, get help, as shouldering all the responsibility for everything can be exhausting. The owner-builder cares about the site and getting the job done, he cares about the people who will be doing it and understands a 'let's get it done' spirit must be created. The owner-builder in his role as site manager and project manager has to demonstrate technical appreciation covering every trade. Rather than count every day, make every day count!

Administrative skills are needed too, as all sorts of records must be kept and information shared between designers and workers. No one else will do it, so have procedures in place that keeps everyone inside the knowledge bubble.

This all needs to be achieved with a light touch, as the team are protective of their status and position on site. If you give an operative some responsibility, make it clear what it is you would like them to be in control of. They should understand what is expected and the quality they should be seeking to deliver. If you make a promise, stick to it, and if they have a grievance, deal with it. Treat all on site equally and fairly. Safety must be enforced in all ways; just because it's not written down, does not mean it's not important.

This is a tall order but the better you perform, the better the result.

Purchasing Policy.

You may think it highfalutin to have something as grand sounding as a purchasing policy. What I mean is a set of rules you follow when purchasing materials for your site. If you do not have any guidelines, you will be firing off orders in an irregular and disorganized fashion, and wasting money. The whole business will be very inefficient. Written orders record what was ordered, delivery notes record what was signed as received, and invoices record costs paid. Knowing your current financial situation is an important tool.

Standard order forms save you time. You will get many repetitive questions each time you place an order, such as: what quantities, what materials, delivery address, order reference, method of payment, delivery date, etc. and a common way to deal with this is to prepare a separate e-mail to each supplier for every order. It is, however, simpler to create a standard order form with a lot of information already included. This purchase order form can also have the ability to include or attach further information and be recognized by a unique order number. This reference is useful when checking orders, deliveries and invoices.

The following points should be included:

- Your name and contact details
- Unique order number and date
- Supplier's name and details
- Full description of material and quantity
- Relevant standard
- Name and manufacturer
- Brand or source of supply
- Brief description of material
- Performance spec if not brand – what standard?
- Cross reference to any relevant drawing
- Agreed price plus discount or rebate
- Delivery date

Note: If suppliers wish to substitute goods or brand, then this can only be acceptable if you have specifically agreed.

Sourcing Goods.

Suppliers fall into two main categories: those regularly purchased from and those you will order from on a single occasion. An example of the first is a timber and general goods supplier, who will provide all sizes and types of wood and associated fixings throughout the works. The second is a skylight supplier, who will deliver to your site on a single occasion.

It may be easier and more cost-effective for you to 'buddy up' with a local general and consumables supplier. Here, you'll give all your purchases to a single business on the understanding that as you will give them a considerable amount of business, they will give you a considerable discount and excellent deliveries. Or you may rather shop around. It's obviously down to what you feel comfortable with.

With your single deal suppliers, as you have never dealt with them before, it is best to be cautious and ensure you have supplied all the correct information. It is worth asking all suppliers what their terms are, e.g. if you have to return goods, will they be subject to a return charge?

Sustainability.

Do you have principles you would like introduced, like material transport miles for goods? Why purchase goods trucked in from many miles away and increase the carbon footprint of your building when you can source goods locally? This leads on to sustainability of the materials purchased. Are you looking for guarantees, certificates or assurances that your timber products are responsibly resourced? Are your external lights moth friendly?

If so, this all becomes part of your purchasing policy.

Quality.

As standard practice, relate the goods ordered to a known quality. Your specification, designer's drawings or web search result will refer to a national standard for almost any product. This sets the level you require the material to meet. For specific items or materials, specifying a proprietary brand, product name and manufacturers' reference number should ensure only selected goods are delivered and not a substituted product. You should state that if changes are made to the material supplied, either in brand or quality then this should only be done after your agreement has been sought and confirmed.

Quantity.

If you are ordering bricks for the footings and external skin of the building, this may well be several full truckloads. To benefit from a discounted price, order all the bricks for the whole job at one time. Ordering the bricks in full loads (possibly mixed loads with engineering and facing bricks) works most efficiently. Get them delivered, one truck at a time, as you need them and you receive the full discount. This allows you to track costs efficiently.

When Needed?

By keeping up-to-date with your schedule of works, you can check with suppliers how much lead-in time is required for a delivery. This tells you when you need to order to have sufficient materials on hand for a contractor on site. This timing can be an art as well as a science as incidents occur and deliveries can be delayed. You must keep in touch with suppliers for updates, particularly on special or one-off purchases. Keep checking all is in order and keep an eye out for any issues that may arise.

Take a leaf from the automotive industry. They championed the 'Just in Time' movement for material deliveries. Meaning, they want them at their plant just when they need them and not before or after.

This has positive benefits:

- Reduces storage space required
- Reduces waste and damage
- Reduces costs as you only pay on or after delivery

I am not suggesting you can get your temporary one-off 'factory' as efficient as a car manufacturer but the principles are worth noting. On tight inner-city lots with minimal storage, this type of thinking can pay dividends.

Design Tweaks.

Be aware that every constructed building has variations from what was originally planned. These changes will alter material requirements in all sorts of ways. When you consider a change, review what other implications it will have on delivery schedules. Often it is an unintended consequence which has the largest affect. Obviously, as it is unintended, it is unplanned, so be alert.

Receiving.

Confirm that you have received the right product, the right quantity and the right prices for all goods. You will soon discover mistakes are common. When you receive goods, have a site-based file (can be either electronic or paper) to safely store all delivery notes. These must be checked off against your order and also checked off against invoices received. It does not matter if you have already paid for the goods in full before delivery. Overcharging can be rectified by good records. This delivery and cost information should be added to your often-updated cost schedule.

Tools and Equipment.

Very few of us think we build too quickly! So it's ideal to think of ways to save time. Activities are definitely speedier using electrical/battery hand tools and mechanical tools and equipment.

The first decision to be made is: what will you use often enough to warrant buying?

We are becoming a throwaway world of almost one-use electric hand tools. Mass-produced products are so cheap they can often be discarded after use and will probably only last for a single project. These discount brands are never as good or long-lasting as quality tools, but do you care?

Larger equipment is another matter. Concrete mixers can be worth purchasing as they are useful items to have around… but consider how regularly a particular piece of equipment will be needed?

You'll need to work through how you will tackle different jobs to work this out. As part of OH&S processes, you now have an understanding of risk assessments. In these, you define what it is you're doing and what material, equipment, access, and labor you will need. By working through this even broadly, you will soon have an idea of requirements.

Tools and equipment purchase is expensive as you need to factor in the original purchase, power costs to operate, and maintenance and repair costs. Hire is expensive too, as the hire companies charge for each day and costs can soon escalate. They often make substantial profits from people forgetting items are on hire and simply racking up invoices.

Security can be an issue too; if you own lots of equipment and tools, you must keep them all safe from theft. By hiring whenever an item is needed, you transfer that security risk to others.

A good balance of purchase and hire is probably the answer for most owner-builders. But be aware of costs as they can soon add up and influence budgets.

On Site Welfare.

Before any works start, you must consider on-site welfare. Measures should be taken to familiarise yourself with your responsibilities according to your local area. Different localities have different requirements and you must ensure the site complies with local OH&S regulations.

Sheds should be installed in preparation for use as a site office or for storage and shelter. Position these in allocated storage areas, and erect any hoardings or security fences.

Temporary toilets should be installed and all in order prior to works commencing. It is prudent to locate them where they will be in the least disruptive position in relation to work areas.

A temporary electrical supply should be connected and made available for site works. You should ensure any required installation certificates are sought and retained, plus re-testing of the temporary supply should be in accordance with OH&S requirements. These set periods should be faithfully followed and any further issued certificates retained.

Boundaries and Grid Lines.

On their working drawings, your designer should set out a series of grid lines to be used as reference points across the site. The first point to be confirmed is clarity on boundaries and other fixed positions. Unless it is very straightforward or you are sufficiently skilled, you should get a land surveyor/setting out engineer or other suitably-qualified person to set out grids around the site. These grids will become your fixed points to take measurements from. If these are correct, your house will be correctly positioned. The opposite is also true!

TRUE STORY

A designer I know came across an 'interesting' situation recently. A builder set out a timber frame house and provided 'hurdles' at each corner with two nails, one for the inside and one for the outside of the walls. When the frame was erected, he noticed that the set-out seemed strange and discovered that the concreter had selected one inside nail and one outside nail on the two long walls. Therefore, the house was rhomboid in shape! That house exists today, 9" (225mm) out of square... hence there are no tiles on the floor, the carpet is very plain and the subsequent owners are slightly puzzled. It would have been easier to have given a single point, say the middle point of the foundation trench and this confusion would have been avoided.

As a rule, simple is always better than complicated.

It is important to get a few points clearly marked a little away from the main build area, which will not be disturbed during works. These will be your check marks as fixed points, always to be returned to for reference as works proceed. It is not unusual for grid lines to be moved or disturbed during works, so these check marks can save a lot of stress down the line.

Also, it is essential you have levels set, so the ground floor level in particular can be established. Marking out levels is crucial to building structures accurately and so a fixed level point as a 'solid' reference is advisable. This should be a fixed point that is unlikely to move. Say, a manhole cover or kerb, ideally, outside of your site/build area. This level point is known as a temporary bench mark (TBM).

Land surveyors will often fix a nail which they will relate back to an ordinance survey level. This will give a value or height for a checkpoint, and it becomes your site datum. This is a crucial point because any level taken can be checked back to this point. Many designers take this point as zero or 100 and every level or height is plus or minus this number.

It is very useful during the build if the surveyor fixes a few other nail points adjacent to your build area to indicate known heights. These heights should be carefully noted (in brightly colored spray paint in large numerals) so on site, a known level point can be easily accessed.

Setting Out.

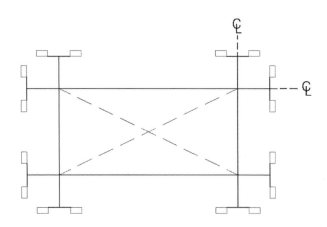

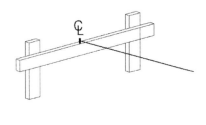

PLAN
STRING LINE INDICATES ℄ OF TRENCHES
DIAGONALS ARE EQUAL IF BUILDING LAYOUT IS SQUARE

HURDLE WITH NAIL FIXED AT
℄ (CENTRE LINE) OF TRENCH

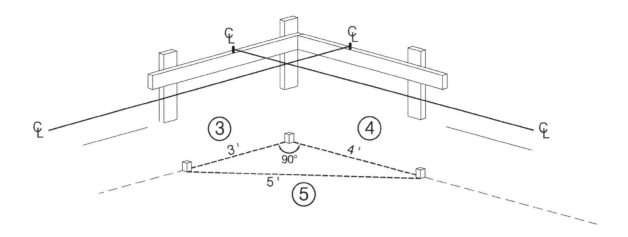

A RIGHT ANGLE OF 90° IS CREATED TO A RATIO OF 3 - 4 - 5

Q. *As it is so important, why not get the surveyor to do the setting out?*

A. Yes, this is what many people do. You prepare the site profiles and erect them, ready for the surveyor. It is very useful to stay on site with the surveyor as you can make alterations and understand what levels and lines he has fixed. The excavator then reduces the levels of the oversite surface so that the build area is prepared and *more* level. It does not have to be perfect but rather improved. Dependant on your foundation plan, you may install some legs of the foundation and commence drainage works.

It is often the case that site profiles that were nicely in place were then moved or destroyed by a machine in what is a robust environment. Trade contractors wanting alternate lines will also be an issue, as will be establishing points in between. Surveyors are accustomed to returning to site. This will cost you a return fee and a time fee, but it can be a worthwhile investment. Obviously, try to employ a reasonably local surveyor.

That said, surveyors returning regularly becomes costly. While surveyors are on site, get as many fixed points as you can, and then get a few more!

Q. *What do you have to do?*

A. Following the designer's drawing, you need to set out the *centerlines* of trenches, so you can instruct the excavator driver as to the line to follow. The profiles are placed opposite each other, so by attaching a string line between the two ends, you can physically tie string along the centerline of the trench. Mark the ground with a brightly-colored line of spray paint as a marker for the excavation. The lines should be central to the excavation dig. As works proceed, keep checking.

The earth will be piled up and removed from site by trucks. Concreters will place steel reinforcement and concrete in the trench foundations. Once done, you must ensure all ground structures are constructed in the correct place. So, it is important the dig is carried out accurately.

If you intend to install a piled foundation, then setting out follows the same process. You need to physically stake position points at the center of each pile.

> **TIP BOX**
>
> *Topsoil Storage*
>
> Topsoil is often cleared off across the site and stored for later re-use in the garden areas on completion. Occasionally check if the topsoil is covered in weeds. If it is, by storing and re-introducing the same soil, you re-introduce the weeds. So, take advice and clear the weeds and/or add nutrients to the soil. Monitor the stockpile and if weeds return, take action.
>
> The time the stockpile is stored also affects the quality of the soil. Before replacement, you may want to run in new, clean topsoil or mulch to improve topsoil quality. Raking or roughening of the under-surface of the ground will improve the soil's cohesion.

Know Your History.

Where there is evidence of previous construction, it's prudent to check into the site history to determine the extent of any previous structures and if any surprises are lurking beneath. No matter how much checking is done, only through excavation can you establish what is underneath the surface. Even when you believe the area is a green field site and always has been, you often uncover old walls and remnants of buildings constructed for agricultural use.

Site Survey.

You need a site survey indicating all topographical features and boundaries. This survey should fix all surface drainage points and any structures remaining, such as walls, gates, garden beds, etc. Sometimes designers incorporate this crucial information onto their drawings but their information is usually taken from initial site surveys. The source document is always preferable.

By comparing the survey with designers' plans, you can determine what needs to be removed off site or stored on-site in order to commence works.

To avoid services conflicts, it is worth marking up a drawing with service runs across the site, including telecommunications and broadband technology. Services are installed at different set depths and suppliers will state how far distant they need to be from each other. Inform the services installers where all the other services are located as damage can occur if the service positions crossover.

Know Your Drawings.

It is in your interest to study all design and engineering drawings, so you are very familiar with all sections and plans. Why? You can only ensure there is no conflicting information by comprehensively knowing how things fit together. Conflicts are where one drawing indicates something at odds with another. At design stage, earlier revisions and small details can be inadvertently left on drawings and errors can creep in.

Consultants generally have standard notes on their information sheets and drawings in an attempt to free them from responsibility, while contractors often try to pass on costs from these conflicts to clients. Picking up questionable points before they are constructed is always the best outcome.

Knowing your construction details and working out which levels things are at is a key part of the owner-builder's role. For example:

- Do drainage layouts indicate a drain needs to pass through a foundation?
- What depth will your manholes be set at?
- Are there retaining walls requiring special support?

If any such items arise, you will need to carefully plan your excavation so works follow an intelligent sequence. Your engineer will have provided you with a foundation plan and the designer with a drainage layout.

Building Information Modelling (BIM) is increasingly an accepted method of providing digital information in many layers. It was originally introduced on larger scale projects and the base drawings are overlaid with various pieces of information. These are viewed in 'layers' so that various positions of structure and services do not try to occupy the same space (or clash). This can be useful, but a high level of IT skills is required and all designers and professionals must have compatible software.

Finished Floor Levels.

Your designer's drawings will have *finished floor levels* (FFL) indicated. It is important you understand what this means. It should mean exactly what it says: the level of the finished floor. However, it is common for mistakes to arise from this point.

Consider what your finished floor is intended to be. If the floor is a structural concrete slab (say a garage), the FFL is often taken as the level of the finished concrete surface. Designers sometimes provide both *structural floor level* (SFL) and FFL. This comes into play where you have a floor covering on top of the SFL (say carpet or tile). This floor covering is referenced as FFL. It can also be indicated that the SFL is under the FFL, which is the floor screed. Confusingly, this screed can be covered with a floor covering.

Are you having a monolithic (single slab) or a structural slab with a screed finish?

Are you placing a floor covering on top of the concrete finish? This could be tile, carpet or a wooden floor.

Establish exactly what level is indicated on the drawing, as all your measurements will come from this point. Obviously, upper floors or split-levels must also be clearly understood. The level of the floor will determine the height of all elements. This includes windows, doors, stairs, etc. and so is crucial.

Trees and Landscaping.

If trees are to remain on completion of the build, you are well advised to protect them with a physical barrier to stop unintentional damage. Wrapping them in a high visibility material (Hi Viz) to alert drivers and machine operators is always good practice. Things best avoided should be highly visible so as to reinforce the message.

Questions to consider:

- Determine if you are to clear away any ground foliage to reduce site levels
- Are you storing topsoil within your own boundary or are you removing it from site?
- Are you disposing of under-surface material?

Whatever the outcome, you will have to organize a mechanical excavator and trucks. Usually, local contractors will advise you on site of the scale and machinery most appropriate. It can be useful to source the mechanical excavator and trucks from the same contact.

It is not unknown for truck drivers to charge waiting time fees if the excavator breaks down. Equally, if no trucks are available or are delayed, you may well incur extra days' hire charges from the machine operator. By having the arrangement with a single contractor, this then becomes their problem and they will usually ensure their unrecoverable costs are minimised.

Reducing site levels is an inexact science yet an expensive one. You must instruct the driver of a mechanical excavator on how much soil to remove. To advise on this, you must precisely understand the position of your building and the depth of your 'dig'. You can judge the position of the outside walls from looking at the grid lines. By placing a laser level to measure from a fixed datum point, you can accurately determine the level of the reduced dig.

Laser Level.

Purchasing your own laser level can be a great tool investment and a real comfort to the harassed manager. It beams a light either horizontally or vertically, thus you can see exactly what level you need and how heights relate to each other.

Using a laser level, you are restricted externally in bright light but generally you can measure around the site somehow. They fit onto tripods and also have magnets fitted so they can be fixed to any secure steel surface.

They are also useful inside the building, helping you to level walls, ceilings, benches, etc.

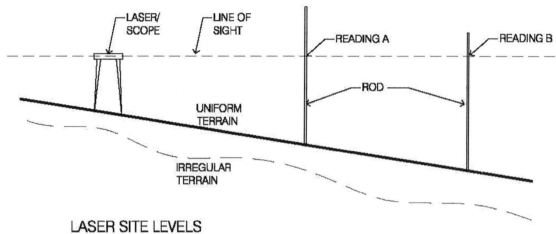

LASER SITE LEVELS
DEDUCT READING 'A' FROM READING 'B' TO DETERMINE THE
AMOUNT OF FALL BETWEEN THE TWO POINTS

Excavation.

Both the engineer and building inspector will check the excavated foundations before they are concreted. This is so they witness that they are clean of loose material and are founded on a solid base. Any reinforcement should be fixed and ready for inspection.

Along similar lines, it is always advisable to maintain your own photographic record as works progress, since you never know what issues may come up in the future.

Make it your mission to be prepared and organized. It is up to you to ensure safe access is provided to work areas, through use of scaffolds or access equipment. Conveniently locate all materials and check workers' operations do not hinder an allied trade.

You must foresee what materials will be required and ensure they are ordered in good time. A late delivery often pushes works out of sequence and this can lead to inefficiency and delay.

Some contractors prefer to supply materials and equipment as well as labor. This can be a good deal for all concerned as they can organize their own material deliveries and equipment. It is also their responsibility to ensure they match operative numbers to the scheduled works. This takes away equipment and material supply issues from you, allowing you more time to manage the site.

Radon.

Ask questions about local site conditions and be aware of possible issues. Parts of Canada and the United States are prone to Radon gas under the earth's surface… is your site in an area of possible risk?

Trucks and Spoil Removal.

A few pointers for excavations and removals are:

Paint clear and large signage indicating known level points to assist understanding by all on site. This can be as simple as an arrow with numerals indicating levels, spray-painted onto a permanent fence or structure. This valuable information will be available throughout the early phases of works.

Ensure a responsible person instructs the machine operators and truck drivers as to when to enter the site. They should visually check that all loads taken from site are full or are as recorded for weight and bulk.

A ticket system, which operates on the basis of a ticket signed for each load taken, is common. So the more tickets signed, the more invoices to pay. It is virtually impossible to dispute the amount of spoil taken from an excavation later as when the spoil is disturbed from its compacted state in the earth, it bulks up. This bulking can be anywhere between 20 and 50 per cent. The onus is on you to ensure that an accurate count of tickets is taken as each load will be expensive and costs can soon escalate.

Always discuss with the machine operating company which machine is most suitable for the work in hand. The machine size makes a vast difference to the speed and efficiency and therefore progress of works. Machine drivers are not usually charged out at a higher rate for different sized vehicles, so all you are paying for is the difference in the actual machine hire.

Equipment hire operators usually charge for the time their machines are on site, not the time they are operating. If delays occur because trucks are not arriving as scheduled, you will pay. Trucks removing spoil will charge a waiting time if they are delayed at your works, and once again, you will pay.

You should be clear on all the check points throughout the build process. An example of this is drains; they require testing to confirm they function correctly.

Who witnesses these tests and what certification must you receive to confirm they have passed the inspection? It is important to know what procedures are to be followed regarding various points in need of visual inspection and testing onsite.

Chapter 5 – Action

- Familiarise yourself with all the drawings
- Set out the grids
- Mark or paint bold, large numbers indicating levels
- Confirm all required inspection points and collect certificates
- Confirm depths and spacings of the incoming services

CHAPTER 6
SUMMARY

Highlights covered in this chapter include:

- What are Building Codes?
- Building Codes are not a choice
- Why a Building Code Certificate or Certificate of Occupancy is important

CHAPTER 6

BUILDING CODES

'Let every man be master of his time'.
– William Shakespeare

Building code approval can seem like pole vaulting. You have a long run up and you have to get over the bar cleanly... a job reserved for the youngest and fittest. It need not be like this, although you may fret at what you have to go through to be judged as 'compliant'.

Building codes have evolved to protect you and everyone else. It lays out standards to be met, and if you meet them, you will have a safe building. If you exceed them, you will have a very safe building and a very well-insulated, eco-friendly home.

Building codes are a set of rules/regulations/laws which, as a minimum, all structures have to meet to comply with local building standards. The regulations are designed to regularize standards you must achieve for every newly built property. Devised by experts, these controls are adopted into state/province law and by local municipalities.

The US and many other countries across the world work with the International Building Code (IBC) and the International Residential Code (IRC). This was developed by the International Code Council (ICC) from legacy codes developed in the eastern, southern and western states of the US.

National Building Code is developed by the Canadian government and local building codes also apply to each province and territory.

Building code compliance is not an area of choice. If you do not comply, you may be told to demolish your non-compliant, and thus deemed dangerous, building. Strict penalties can also be raised. The local city has authority to take action to make safe or even demolish dangerous structures without your agreement. These laws are in place to protect anyone who interacts in any way with the building.

Each jurisdiction has, at a minimum, their own codes. Due to the costs involved with developing and updating standards, a national standard is adopted, with perhaps a local twist to meet a special condition. It is not a purpose of the codes to promote any particular types of design or construction.

It is the purpose of codes to insist on set standards of construction and design. This acts to keep buildings safe for their occupants, make buildings comfortable to use, and provide access for all. Codes are also produced to stop structural or equipment failure and encourage energy saving through high levels of insulation.

Building code approval is often required before construction can commence and is considered as part of the build permit application. Standards are applied to different aspects of the build process, some more advanced and stringent than others. You should seek advice from your designer or your local building control department as to what has to be done in your area to comply with building control.

Zone Permit, Build Permit Versus Building Code Control.

It is important to distinguish between zone and build permits and building codes. Zone and build permits give you permission to construct the structure as indicated on the set of approved drawings to a certain height and mass and they will have looked at building code compliance. However, if you do not need a zone or build permit, this does not exempt you from building code control or complying with other applicable laws. They are quite separate and the overriding issue is that you construct everything to a minimum code standard.

Process.

The building process is there to approve the method and structural integrity of the build. The design and construction must comply with all aspects of the building or code regulations. Your team must establish compliance with structural stability, drainage, smoke detection, spread of fire controls, access for people with a disability and emergency services, ventilation, stairways, ramps and guards, electrical, plumbing, roofing, environmental and fuel conservation matters, demolition of existing structures and other related issues. So what does this process involve?

During the construction period, certain stages need to be physically inspected and passed as meeting the standard. This is done in an on-site visit by the building inspector. These are usually inspections of foundations, reinforcement, drainage, services, insulation, roofing, etc. If you do not inform and invite the inspector to check the onsite situation, he can require you to open up the works for inspection to prove compliance. It is worth confirming and listing these build stages so that you do not inadvertently complete works and cover them before they are inspected and approved.

Inspections.

If at all possible, it is good to personally attend all inspections so you can directly discuss the on-site situation without the filter of an operative or contractor, who may not like what they hear or accurately pass on critical or crucial information.

It is important you understand exactly what is said as this feedback will directly affect further works that may need to be carried out. The issue of permits/certificates are dependent on approval that will only be issued after it has been assessed that your works offered as complete comply with the building codes.

Much of the information needed to ensure you comply with building codes is available online or can be ascertained by a visit to your local municipality offices.

Utility suppliers may require other documentation and drawings before allowing you to commence works close to their services.

Changes to Building Codes.

The evolving threat of climate change has led to many changes and re-interpretations of building codes. The codes are becoming stricter, not easier, to meet as environmental changes are recorded as affecting all properties, new or old. In the past 20 years, many new records have been set for the driest, wettest, hottest, most destructive years, etc. in all parts of the world and these changes are having a huge impact on our local conditions. Building regulations are regularly updated to meet these challenges.

In the main, this is in relation to the materials used to manufacture products and to the levels of CO^2 and carbon footprint they create. It is widely predicted that codes will also be upgraded to meet the challenge of increasingly frequent weather-related super-storms.

Other changes are introduced to meet fears and concerns of fire or serious illness. Buildings must be designed to be as safe as possible for their constructors and later residents. Stringent fire controls are adopted to reduce the opportunity of fire, or if it does occur, to loudly warn residents of the danger and allow them to escape to safety. Certain building materials are banned, due to the danger of constructors coming into contact with it or breathing in noxious fibers or chemicals.

U-Values.

U-values are an important talking point and relate to the coefficient of thermal transmittance. In simpler terms, it gives a value to the ease of transmission of heat through a material.

Insulation values in the home are taken seriously; building codes require that minimum standards of insulation are met in all the external features. Walls, roofs, ground floors, windows, skylights, and doors all need to meet a required standard. While the 'required standard' is also the minimum standard to meet building codes, manufacturers also produce improved and premium products which exceed the set minimums.

Why not improve on these standards and reduce U-values throughout your home? This will translate into energy savings, which in turn will lower energy bills.

Remember – a lower U-Value, is more efficient.

In summary, building code control is locally driven and you must comply or you may not receive a building completion/occupancy certificate or insurance cover. The lack of these documents will have ramifications if you ever decide to sell the property, or much sooner, when you go to take out a home mortgage.

In some areas, stringent fines may be levied for each day a system is not compliant.

TRUE STORY

I was once asked to assist to diagnose a mystery water stain in the middle of a top floor wall. We inspected the *copings* and they appeared to be properly installed, with a damp-proof course (DPC) visible on both edges under the coping stones. We tracked down every point on the roof where there may have been a weakness but were left puzzled. It became obvious that we needed an intrusive survey, so we started removing wall plaster and ceilings to trace the problem back to its source. On removing a section of coping, we found the DPC was in place but rather than a single DPC across the top of the wall, the bricklayer had installed two strips that did not meet in the middle. This gave an opening for moisture; water always follows the easiest course.

The water stain did not show locally (at the point of ingress) but halfway across the building!

Why did the bricklayer install something as important as a DPC incorrectly?

I believe it was because he wanted to progress the works and did not want the delay of getting the correct DPC. It suited him to move ahead and he probably thought the DPC as he installed it would be OK.

Had he flagged up that he was short of material a day earlier, the correct material could have been made available.

Had he said he was delayed on the day, he could have worked on an adjacent wall for an hour or taken an early lunchbreak while the correct DPC was purchased and delivered.

The cost and hassle associated with the repair far outweighed any gain of him taking a chance and installing the incorrect material.

Lesson: Always check all trades have the correct material to hand each and every day.

Certificates.

You will have to present a full series of certificates of compliance at the end of the project in order to be issued with a Building Code Certificate or a Certificate of Occupancy. Prepare by determining before commencement what is on the list so that you can methodically collect them as works proceed.

It is not simply a box checking exercise. You should not try to substitute building control and its steps for solid on-site management. It is your responsibility to ensure all construction works are completed to the highest standards and passed by the building inspector. Remember inspectors will only certify what they have personally witnessed.

The issuance of the *Building Code Certificate or Certificate of Occupancy* is important, not least because it demonstrates your home is complete and suitable for occupation. The certificate's issue can be relied upon as a defining point in time, which may be useful. For example, you may wish to demonstrate the date when the works were complete. The issue of this certificate will provide this evidence.

Chapter 6 – Action

- Discuss the building control code in your area with your designers
- Find out what certificates are required and start collecting them as works proceed
- Keep reinforcing the importance of building to the plan details provided, to everyone who will listen
- Consider upgrading the levels of insulation to the whole house

CHAPTER 7
SUMMARY

Excavations are one of the main items where caution is required and due consideration is necessary.

Highlights covered in this chapter include:

- What hazards lie under the surface
- Safe Working Method Statement (SWMS)
- Search before you dig

CHAPTER 7

EXCAVATIONS

'Where there is muck, there is money'.
— Unknown

Excavations are Inherently Dangerous and Costly

This statement is worth highlighting, as works below ground level can be fatal to workers, are expensive when correctly carried out, and horrendously expensive when incorrectly carried out. As excavation works are only ever a means to doing other things, it seems that insufficient attention to details is often the case. For instance, only by removing soil can you fill trenches with concrete for a foundation. The foundation supporting the building usually becomes the focus, not how the excavations are safely carried out.

As so many opportunities for injury present themselves during the groundworks process, owner-builders should carefully consider the works and how they are tackled. Owner-builders have a duty of care to everyone who comes in the briefest of contact with his site or build project. This includes all workers, visitors, delivery people, consultants or neighbors. By following good practice and building codes, you should achieve compliance and avoid identifiable hazards.

What about unidentified hazards? You must consider all risks associated with the works, not only those covered by building codes. Unidentified hazards can still cause grief for all involved. It is vital that you are aware of what may happen, even if you have not formally recognized that risk by way of a mitigation plan.

Compliance is not the sole aim; the main aim is to have nil accidents and a safe site for all. Anything short of this will put you at risk. As discussed in the OH&S chapter, self-preservation as well as preservation of others is a real concern. Failures may occur without warning and at such speed that operatives are unable to escape an extensive collapse.

No matter who is in charge of excavations, an owner-builder or a specialist contractor, excavation exceeding 5' 0" (1.5m) deep is considered 'high risk construction work'. This is quite a low threshold; trenches or retaining walls often exceed this height. Responsibility is spread around but primary responsibility remains with owner-builders as the person in charge of the enterprise.

TRUE STORY

> In Boston MA, a fire hydrant supply pipe running adjacent to a trench got damaged and flooded the trench so quickly that two workers drowned. It was found that the company owner had been reckless with the OH&S and he was sentenced to three years in prison. Preparation and planning can save lives.

Planning Excavation Works.

Planning excavations usually start after geotechnical and structural engineers have considered the soil conditions and designed the foundations. This is your starting point, along with the site survey and the architectural designer's scheme. This will, when taken together, show you the amounts and areas to be excavated. Your part is deciding how the spoil is safely excavated; how it is piled up and disposed of.

Trucks coming and going from site can be disruptive to neighbors, as well as spread muck from their wheels rolling away on local roads. Usually at the planning application stage, you must develop a proposal to address these points by stating how you will marshal the trucks, how many loads a day you intend to remove, and what wheel washing facilities will be available. It is a comprehensive traffic management plan. A requirement or not, it is good practice to consider these points and institute your site policy.

> **TIP BOX**
>
> *Consideration for excavations*
>
> Ground conditions
> Weather conditions
> SWMS
> Existing services
> How will equipment and trucks enter site?
> The length of time the excavations are open to the elements
> Loads near the excavations
> Adjacent buildings

Excavations are opened up to enable foundations and retaining walls to be installed. Whatever the design, you will want the opening and foundation installation to be seamless. If banks of earth are left exposed, they will collapse after inclement weather. Trenches need to be secure and firm in preparation to install reinforcement steel, drains and concrete.

Adjacent buildings must be protected against any of your works. If you are excavating close to them, you must have an engineer's design already agreed with your neighbor's professional representatives. This can be by a party wall agreement or an informal agreement. Your neighbor will decide if a formal agreement is needed. Excavation works can seriously affect the stability of nearby buildings and so they must be protected from subsidence or vibration. This work should be carried out by competent people, taking special care so that no water penetrates adjacent buildings.

Underground Service Routes.

Owner-builders must establish the likelihood and location of current underground services and make all operatives aware of their existence. If services are 'live' or may cross areas of excavation, you must first liaise with service suppliers who have this information available and offer a 'dial before you dig service'. Records of the locations of services on your lot can be inaccurate or out of date and so caution when digging is necessary.

This caution applies equally to overhead services, where strict control measures should be in place to prevent any machines coming into any form of contact with live lines. The relevant suppliers will advise on safe working distances and appropriate measures to be instituted. Arcing can occur where an electrical current 'jumps' across an air space and connects with an object, especially a highly conductive metal like an excavator or a scaffold. So be aware that you do not need to touch an electrical cable to receive an electrical charge.

Security.

It is the owner-builder's responsibility to secure excavation works against unauthorised entry. You must consider the likelihood of unauthorised entry; not only from a road, but from people crossing local parks, schools, etc. and the risks such an entry can throw up. This is not an easy call to make, but you must be aware of the danger.

Spoil.

The concern is that the excavated spoil is stored too close to the trench and it falls back, refilling the trench and burying workers. To avoid this, excavated spoil should be moved away and not stored in the 'zone of influence' (ZOI), which is adjacent to excavated trenches. The exact details of the ZOI can only be established by a geotechnical engineer, but it's often considered to be a 45 degree angle taken from the lowest excavated area in an unsupported trench. It can be closer if trench supports have been designed and installed. On a sloping site, make sure spoil is stored on the lower side of the excavation, as gravity will come into play and slippage becomes more likely. Ensure water runoffs are channelled so as to direct it away from excavations.

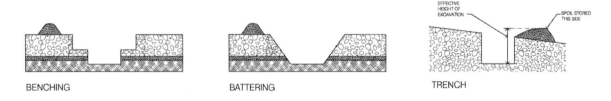

SAFE EXCAVATIONS

On sites with limited space, trucks can often be driven close to an excavated area. The engineer/designer will have ensured the design calls for increased propping and trench support to meet these imposed loads. The engineer also considers saturated soils and ground water pressures.

Benching & Battering.

Benching is the creation of steps designed to reduce the height of the excavation walls locally. This prevents possible collapse by excavating to different horizontal levels. *Battering* is created by sloping the sides of the excavation so that the effect of any collapse would be restricted and minimised. Benching and battering can be combined in the same excavation.

Shoring.

Shoring is a ground support system, which relies on the steel or timber shoring. The engineer will produce a ground condition-appropriate design and the SWMS documentation will reflect this.

The system's purpose is to support the excavated faces to prevent collapse and thus allow safe working conditions. The shoring must be installed as works proceed and not installed on completion. This is so a collapse does not occur before the support system is in place. Operatives should not enter any unsupported part of the excavation.

Steel supports are becoming more popular than timber as they are more flexible and can be adjusted to support different widths of trenching.

Trench Sheeting.

The trenching sheets are held up and driven into the ground to a designed depth. This work can be carried out by attachments to mechanical excavators or by hand-held pneumatically-driven hammers. The sheets should be placed in position vertically and true, as each adjoining sheet will overlap and connect, making a solid face.

Steel sheet piling is mostly used in deeper trenches. This is to retain a bank of earth or where someone is intending to excavate near existing buildings. Steel support trench is not as heavy as standard sheet piling. This work is noisy and the SWMS should recommend hearing protection equipment.

Removal of shoring can be as dangerous as installation and this should also be carefully planned and carried out. To avoid removal work, sheets are sometimes left in position as sacrificial formwork. The sheets are simply left behind.

Biodegradable formwork sheets are also on the market. If the engineer considers the site has 'reactive' soil, they may want a void formed around the foundation. Reactive soils are clay-type soils that swell and shrink in different weather conditions. Biodegradable sheets will, in the natural course of events, degrade and leave the void in place.

Regular Inspection.

Weather conditions can quickly change and regular inspections, particularly after heavy rain, are advisable. The state of the ground behind the shores can swell or slip and water courses can become apparent. Where necessary, ensure repairs or re-strengthening takes place before works continue.

It is good practice to dig in a *sump* at a low point of the excavation. Inclement weather does regularly occur and water can fill the bottom of excavations. Water will naturally drain to the lowest point and effective pumping can take place.

Safe Work Method Statement (SWMS).

The recommended way of demonstrating you have considered risks is by preparing a *Safe Work Method Statement* (SWMS) and issuing this document to the workforce. This is not mandatory in all areas but can do you no harm; in fact, it can do a lot of good. This document should describe the works, labor, materials, equipment and recommend control measures.

Issuing safety documents does not excuse you of liability. You must follow up on the statement, ensuring all its recommendations are followed. In addition, you must keep reviewing all OH&S issues and method statements as works proceed. You cannot just file documents away and feel secure in the knowledge you are covered. If a specialist contractor is managing the excavations, they should supply a SWMS to you. In the event of a serious incident, you will then have these documents recording your instructions and showing how you intended the works to be carried out.

In the real world of a single house owner-builder instructing a self-employed ground worker, this all may seem like it is over-the-top and beyond what on-site conditions call for. Be aware, though, in the event of an accident, you will be relentlessly grilled by officials and lawyers asking very serious questions.

Emergency Planning.

An emergency plan in the case of earth slippage or flooding should be added to the methodology. This will give a ready answer should you need to contact emergency services following an incident. This should also be incorporated into the whole site OH&S documents.

Chapter 7 – Action

- Determine if your foundation trenches are designed to exceed 5'0" (1.5m) depth
- Write and issue a SWMS
- Plan vehicle access to the site area
- Batter spoil by trenches
- Dig a sump

MONEY/TIME
Budget & Cash Flow
Finance Timings
Pay Contractors/Suppliers

DESIGN
Collect Certificates - Ongoing
Seek Quotations

WORKS
On Going Building Control Inspections
Meet Contractors
Appoint Contractors

CHAPTER 8
SUMMARY

Services are necessary for all homes, decide what you will have and what you will not.

Highlights covered in this chapter include:

- Temporary power supplies
- Stand Alone Power (SAP)
- Solar PV and battery systems
- Heating systems
- Layout service points on plans
- Layout of power points and lighting

CHAPTER 8

EXTERNAL INFRASTRUCTURE AND HOME SERVICES

'We will make electricity so cheap that only the rich will burn candles'.
– Thomas A. Edison

Services power homes and enable them to function. The services available are determined by the location of the site, but which services you choose from those available are down to you. Installation costs for some services can be expensive although some are subsidized by your state or province and so installation costs can vary substantially

Infrastructure

Infrastructure services are commonly installed by utility companies; in other words, large companies with a monopoly for their installation. In some areas, the delivery is split between an infrastructure-only company and suppliers who retail the service to householders. Almost all new homes rely on mains distributed sources of energy.

Electricity.

With the increasing efficiency of electrical generating systems and decreasing costs of this equipment, in remote circumstances it can, be advantageous to install a Stand Alone Power System (SAPS). These systems are not supported by mains electricity systems and so are off grid.

Stand Alone Power Systems are confusingly referred to as:

- Stand Alone Power System (SAPS)
- Standalone Power Systems (SPS)
- Remote Area Power Supply (RAPS)
- Micro Power Systems (MPS)

These acronyms all describe the same thing.

Systems usually have more than one method of generating electricity. Often the system is a combination of solar panels and wind turbine, with generated power stored in a linked bank of batteries. A petrol/diesel/biofuel generator can be a useful back up. Heating homes with geothermal sources and heat pumps are also options in some areas.

The benefits of an SAPS are: the provider can save resources by not stringing a set of power poles across the country to link a single home up to the grid, and by installing a SAPS, you can be as 'green' as you wish.

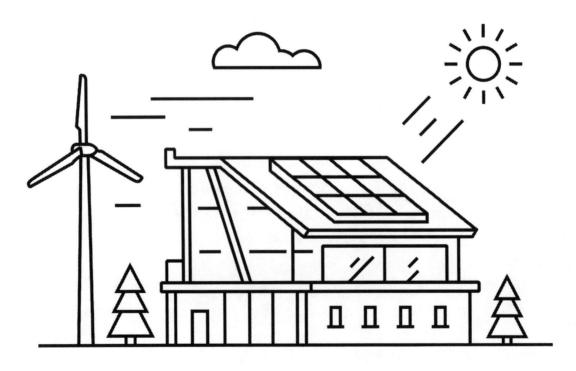

One bonus of purchasing an existing house and land for demolition and new construction is very often, mains services already connected. If you are purchasing a vacant block, you must establish the status of local services and costs of connection. The costs associated with introducing services can be substantial and therefore large savings can be achieved if you are able to connect to existing services.

The local electricity supplier takes power from the electrical grid, supplied from the nearest power station or electricity generator. A mains supply is taken into the property and terminates at a *head* position. The head is connected to a meter. Up to this point, the supply is the responsibility of the electrical supply company.

Domestic properties are supplied with a single-phase main supply of 120V. This is not an absolute voltage and is only approximate as the distance of your meter from the power station and local substations vary actual supply voltages.

With the advent of electric cars, it can be prudent to upgrade the supply pressure and flow (Voltage and Amperage) to allow for fast charging. Interestingly, improving battery technology may also allow for the car's battery to store energy for use within the house. So, the house can give to the car and the benefit can be returned.

Types of Electrical Current.

Electricity has two types of current:

- Direct (DC). DC is a current flowing in a single direction
- Alternating Current (AC) is a current which reverses direction many times a second

AC is used in domestic premises and DC is used in digital electronics and both of these types of current are always isolated from each other. Solar panels produce DC power and this is converted to AC by an inverter or microinverter.

Voltage is an electromotive force (EMF). The voltage moves power along cables. The greater or higher the force, the greater or higher the voltage.

Your first point of responsibility as the household occupier will be a service panel aka breaker box, aka distribution board. The distribution board is the place that the external power cables enter after the meter and it acts as a distribution point for all your electrical circuits and location of protection breakers.

The service panel is connected to the household meter by the electrical supplier only once your system is complete and certified by a competent person. This is usually your installation electrician. This certificate confirms compliance with electrical regulations.

The service panel controls the electricity supply entering the property and can turn the electricity supply on or off. It protects the occupants from electrical shock and prevents fires from an electrical fault by automatically closing down the circuit at fault. Each circuit is collectively protected by a single main fuse, which closes down the entire system. This is by either residual current devices (RCDs) or arc fault circuit interrupters (AFICs) aka Arc Fault Detection Devices (AFDDs). Discuss the appropriate circuit protectors for your installation with your electrician.

Circuit Layout.

Layout of lighting and power points is something worth going over in detail, once the design has been frozen.

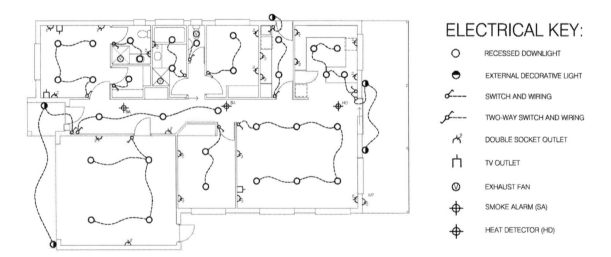

Power Point Layouts.

You need to imagine, as indicated in the program, not only what a room will use electrically but also what else it will be used for. Mark up a clean set of drawings with your intended points and consider which equipment you wish to use. Many items produced are powered by batteries, which need regular charging. You may include more outlet points to make regular plugging in and unplugging unnecessary. By pinpointing each power point and light point on a drawing detailing the number of points and switching (single switch or double switch) a planned distribution of cables and circuits can be installed, which saves extension cords trailing around the home.

Lighting Layout.

The aim is not to evenly light all spaces or individual rooms but rather to use light fittings to enhance the quality of space. Each room should be considered separately and a view taken on what lighting you would like there. For example, bedrooms can be dimly lit when you are retiring and bright when you are dressing or cleaning. Do you want to be able to turn off ceiling lights from the bed or do you prefer wall fixed side lamps?

Dimmers can play a large role as they can allow areas to be dimmed or highly lit, depending on the time of day and use of the room. Works of art or special features can be highlighted with LED strips. LED light fittings also give opportunities to light with color.

Your electrician will provide a *Circuit Chart* which he will fix close to the distribution board. Circuit charts are very useful when an issue arises and individual or groups of power points or lights do not work. A clear and accurate chart of what is on which circuit can be of help with identification, in a stressful fault-finding situation.

Guide - Minimum Number of Double Sockets Per Area

Area Type	Smaller Rooms up to $12m^2$/ $130ft^2$	Medium Rooms 12-$25m^2$ / $130ft^2$-$270ft^2$	Large Rooms Exceed $25m^2$/$270ft^2$
Main Living Area	4	6	8
Bedroom	2	4	5
Office	4	5	6
Laundry	3	4	5
Kitchen	6	8	10
Garage	2	3	4
Hallway	1	2	3
Loft/Basement - Storage	1	2	3

> **TIP BOX**
>
> *Check 1st Fix.*
>
> After the 1st fix electrical installation is offered as complete, it is worthwhile walking through the house and methodically checking the location of each and every power point and light point on the system. This check will confirm the actual location *as fitted* of each point. If necessary, minor amendments can be made before follow-on trades make access and subsequent changes difficult.

Emergency Lighting.

Emergency lighting is not normally required in domestic premises by codes, but this should be confirmed with your building inspector. Even if they are not required, emergency lights are a safety feature worth considering. Emergency light fittings are widely available, with lamps which operate as normal fittings when the power to them is connected and functioning. Should they become isolated (by say a MCB fault or mains power failure), they have an internal battery to power the fitting while the power source is non-operational. They are therefore effective for basic illumination or on emergency escape routes, such as stairs.

Services Within the Home.

Apps are now common for all home services and this movement is driven by rapid technological innovation, ecology, economy and design. Technologies are increasingly marketed with the idea of making the house 'smarter'. This is driven by the recognition we humans are using up natural resources at an alarming rate. If we can help the planet, then all well and good. The new products usually promise energy-saving features, ecological benefits and are aesthetically pleasing, so it seems a win-win.

This may be the case or it may not. Manufacturers endeavour to bring all sorts of additional features and smart tech to previously straightforward products. It's good marketing sense for them to differentiate their product in the marketplace... but does this help you? These features can appear to be awe-inspiring but sometimes they seem unnecessary. An analogy in the household is perhaps the washing machine; they all come with variable spins and multiple wash settings, but how many different settings do you regularly use?

Photovoltaics (PV) / Solar Power.

PV/Solar power to the family home has moved from alternative to mainstream. It has become a mature industry, with established manufacturers and installers plus its own codes of conduct and certification. Detailed and comprehensive guarantees are available both for components and installation.

Solar technology is fast moving; improving battery power for storage is an exciting prospect for reducing reliance on fossil fuels. Solar systems can be retrofitted but are best planned into the project from the outset. Increasing panel efficiency has shown benefits, even where panels do not face directly into the sun.

PV is an electrical generation system of linked solar panels, which converts light energy into electricity to supply electrical power to your home. PV is a very popular method of providing electricity from renewable sources, thus reducing the need to use fossil fuels. From a financial standpoint, the actual efficiency of a particular system depends on your geographic location, the solar panels' access to unshaded sunlight and the internal efficiency of the system.

You do not need to be off-grid to enjoy the benefits of generating your own electricity. You can save money by powering your home (or items in your home) and not paying for electricity from the mains supplier. In some areas, state or central government provide grants to assist with installation costs and pay you (indirectly) for the power you send back to the grid. Depending on location, number of panels and use, these two savings can eliminate electrical bill payments altogether.

Before getting excited at this prospect, you should check both the cost to purchase electricity and the amount you will be paid to provide energy to the grid. It is usually the case that you are not paid as much to provide energy to the grid as you pay to receive energy. Calculating how much electricity you will use and how much you will generate is an art as well as a science. This point can be discussed with solar contractors, who may provide general indications. Or there are various websites and apps with live calculators, many which allow you to specify your geographical location details.

With developing technologies, it can pay you to wait and see, as next year's system will be bigger, better and cheaper. Although it appears that with solar panels and systems, technological advances are incremental, as opposed to major, and prices are flatlining. There are experimental 'printed' solar cells that are in the development stage but they are still some way off from replacing silicon based panels.

Most systems have a payback period of between five to eight years, and this seems to meet the 'reasonable' test for most consumers. After all, systems produce savings for over 25 years. Many solar panels are guaranteed for 25 years and inverters guaranteed for 10 years.

There are also the environmental aspects, with many people preferring to generate clean electricity and reduce society's dependence on fossil fuel or nuclear-powered energy. A 5 kilowatt solar PV system produces enough energy for 50 per cent usage in a typical home every day, if wisely used.

It is beneficial to set timers on your electricity usage. You can set machines or water heaters to commence at the most likely time your system will be generating power, usually the middle of the day.

This does not mean each house is self-sufficient, as energy is purchased and used at times when solar power is not generated. Panels may not work adequately if shaded or on cloudy/rainy days and will not work at all after dusk. To use solar power at these times, you must have first stored enough electricity in specially designed batteries.

Payback Period depends on:

- Your geographic location
- Which direction panels can practically be faced?
- How much shade covers your panels?
- The angle of the panel (improved by frames)
- Size of your system
- Feed-in restrictions to the grid
- Quality of panels and equipment purchased
- Electricity prices from the mains supplier
- Feed-in tariff rates you receive as an electricity generator to the grid
- If you use electrical equipment at the most suitable time of the day

Other things to consider are:

Which inverter will you need/select?
Can you measure the outputs from your system or individual panels?

Are batteries are a good fit for your system?

Gas.

Many homes use piped natural gas for heating and cooking purposes. Natural gas may not be available outside metropolitan areas, where it was not economical for the supply companies to develop the necessary infrastructure.

A gas service is supplied by the gas supply company, or in some areas, a separate infrastructure company. They will advise you how far within your boundary they will take their service and advise on a gas meter location and enclosure.

Up to the meter, the service is in the ownership of the infrastructure company. Your gas fitter (plumber) will take his service from your side of the meter and install pipes to the service points. Gas services are heavily regulated and must comply with local codes of practice regarding acceptable types of service pipes and ventilation. Therefore, you must go over this with your designer and your gas fitter. On completion, you will require a gas safety installation certificate, issued by a gas registered contractor as part of the building control approval requirements.

Gas is going out of favor as many national governments are trying to reduce their reliance on fossil fuels. Government bodies commonly consider proposals from environmental groups calling for a gas ban for installations to new buildings as part of the contribution to global warming reduction. If considering gas, you should check on the attitudes of your government and state for any upcoming prohibitions for new installations and also envisage the increasing cost of natural gas.

In most cases, natural gas is piped to the residence. In off-grid locations, if gas is used, it is supplied in bottles. Gas is popular as an energy source for cooking and can be an efficient form of heat and to fire hot water systems.

Gas is highly volatile and should only be worked on by qualified operatives. Some areas require gas services to enter the building externally, in a ventilated environment. Without consideration and planning, this can lead to unsightly brightly-colored pipes running externally on the face of the building.

Water.

All new homes should be connected to a clean supply of fresh water. Depending on your location, this may be a mains supply if the infrastructure is in place or a private well, if it is not.

Mains water is supplied by an infrastructure company and is taken to a turn off point close to, or on, your property. It is normal for your supply to be metered as a water saving and cost saving exercise. Your plumber will take the water supply pipe from your side of the water meter and run an incoming service to all the outlet points.

The water main to your property would usually be through a 1"/1$^{1/4}$" (25/32mm) diameter polythene pipe. This water service will be pressurised and as such will rise to two, three or more storeys without a pump. The program should determine what water usage your house will require at certain points but not how it is pushed around the building or what storage capacity you shall have, if any at all.

So, you should discuss these issues carefully with your designers and your plumber. Each house can have a combination of solutions, for water distribution and water heating. In general, water is used for kitchens, bathrooms, laundries, gardens, and perhaps garages and sheds.

Where hot water is used as a method of home heating, it is increasingly delivered by combination boilers, which are boilers supplying both hot water for consumption and heating. They heat water instantly, from cold, and do not require storage tanks.

In larger homes, hot water storage tanks are used to store heated water for supply purposes. Pay particular attention to 'dead legs', to see how they can be reduced. These refer to the distance warmed water travels to get to your tap. Often in bathrooms, the basin hot water does not initially reach you warmed up, as you have to run cold water from the dead leg pipe section before the warm water arrives.

Legionella.

Legionella can grow in a water system within the home. Be aware of it and minimise the risk of it spreading and causing infection. The best deterrent is designing out the likelihood of it occurring.

What is it?

Legionella is a bacterium that grows and spreads in a water based system. The disease is a very serious type of pneumonia.

Where would you find it?

- Shower heads, faucets and thermostatic mixing valves.
- Hot tubs – especially spa types that have water left remaining in the circulation system.
- Water fountains and water features.
- Hot water tanks and heaters.
- Large plumbing systems.

How can you avoid it?

- Do not have warm stagnant water left in a system. This can be in the pipework or fittings. Dead legs or slow flow of water is to be avoided.
- The most dangerous point of legionella growth is water held between the temperatures of 68 degrees F (20 degrees C) and 113 degree F (45 degrees C).
- Checking water outlets that are furthest away from the incoming point as they may not have the same levels of town water chlorination.
- Cold water storage tanks particularly in warm climates are liable to the bacteria.
- Thermostatic valves that are set to provide warm water at a temperature that allows bacteria growth.

What can I do?

- Weekly flushing of unused outlets.
- Flush all water outlets if the system has not functioned for a period over 1 week.
- Speak to your installer to confirm the temperatures of the water in the system to ensure it is not within the danger zone.
- Do not breathe in droplets while you are flushing the system.
- Do not panic but just be aware of legionella!

Wells.

If there is no available public water main, a private well can be bored. Private wells are not metered but permission is often required before a private well can be drilled and connected. The water from a private well will need to be tested and approved as complying with public health standards before it can be used for human consumption. A filter/steriliser may be required. You should check the laws in your local area in this regard.

On completion of the project, you may well require a certificate to confirm compliance of the water service for building control purposes.

Heating.

The first decision needed is, the power source for the heating system. Common sources of heating are natural gas and electricity. The installation and appliances' costs associated with these two power sources are the most economical to purchase up-front but the most expensive to run. The move to lower household carbon footprints and provision of ecologically 'sound' installations by utility companies raises some issues and questions over how green the power sources are.

Along with economy and earth friendliness, heating systems should be investigated for efficiency of service. All types of heating systems are available everywhere, but local understanding is a valid issue when it comes to installation and maintenance.

Your geographical location will indicate which heating system is found to work well in your climate. In the UK and Northern Europe, hydronic, water-based heaters are popular and in Southern Europe, US, Canada, New Zealand and Australia, heated air systems find favor. It is important you consider the system which is best in your circumstance.

What is usually required is a system that will heat water all year round, and also in cooler seasons it will increase the ambient air temperature in the living areas of the home. In warmer weather, you may want no heating at all or you may want air cooling.

> **TIP BOX**
>
> Diversity
>
> Diversity is a term often mentioned by plumbers, but what does it mean?
>
> The diversity of a system questions how many fittings/points will call for hot water at the same time?
>
> Most homes are designed cost-effectively and a limited number of simultaneous calls for hot water are allowed for as 'reasonable'. You do not want to waste money by oversizing a system and equally you do not want a system that does not deliver sufficient hot water when required. This is usually only a concern at peak usage time. The design needs to be a blend of an economically designed system that can cope with your families demands for instant hot water.

The water heating system is invariably either stored heated water or instantaneously heated water. Storing water and maintaining it at a suitable temperature is expensive as it must remain constantly heated.

Instantaneous water heating is more economical but is subject to inefficiencies if too many points are calling for hot water at the same time. Larger homes with multiple bathrooms may call for water at similar times and so they tend to have stored water systems, while smaller homes and apartments with less demand tend to have instantaneous water heaters.

Heat Pumps.

Heat pumps are becoming more popular as a modern clean energy source, with competing manufacturers bringing this ever-evolving technology to the market. Heat pump systems are best planned from the early stages of the build as they are not suited to late inclusion.

Heat pumps take heat from their surroundings, either air or from geothermal heat. Air heat pumps are simpler to install and change air taken from the external areas to create heating or cooling.

Central Heating aka Hydronic Heating.

Gas-fired central heating is very common in Europe and is a circulating hot water system pumped around the home through radiators and towel rails, which emit heat. The system can be either a pressurised system or one relying on a gravity-fed tank.

Gas-fired boilers can heat water for storage, and heating can be extracted indirectly, through a heating element inside the cylinder. Direct heating is also widely available: directly from a boiler. A gas-fired system can be very efficient, especially when linked to a water circulating solar heating system.

Condensing Boilers.

Many areas require all newly-installed gas boilers to be 'condensing boilers'. These boilers are more efficient than standard boilers as they re-claim latent heat, which would otherwise have escaped. This type of boiler is designed to drip condensed water vapor and so must be placed where runoff can occur without inconvenience. These boilers run from mains pressure and so can be a benefit if a higher-pressure shower is appreciated, without the added cost of a water shower pump.

Underfloor Heating.

Underfloor heating systems are popular as they cleverly deliver heat to the home through the floor structure. They are not a quick fix if you are feeling cold as they have a time lag from activation until you feel the benefit. So, these systems are best suited as a background heat, maintaining a level temperature. Underfloor heating can be powered by electric, natural gas or air pumps, and each power source is earmarked as the most suitable according to location.

One standout feature is the heaters (pipes) are hidden by the floor covering and so the emitters (radiators) do not compete for wall space or have floor grilles which cannot be covered over.

Forward planning is important as some areas of floor do not benefit from unremitting heat. This is the case beneath kitchen units, where food or perishable items may be stored, or under refrigerators, where you are heating an appliance that's expending energy to get cooler.

Electric Panel Heaters.

Electric panel heaters come in two types, but confusingly they are regularly misnamed. They are known as panel heaters, convection heaters or electric radiators. Technically, only heaters which primarily radiate heat should be called radiators, with all others considered to be convection heaters or emitters. Radiated heat is delivered with heat from the radiator directly heating the person or object and the air between. Convection is heating the air, which then secondarily heats the person or air.

Electric Radiators use a combination of radiated heat and convected heat and are more efficient than a heater simply convecting. Generally, radiators are more expensive so it is best to place them in areas which more often have people to heat and convectors placed in less used spaces.

Air Systems.

Air systems are forced air conditioning, heating and cooling systems which introduce external air into the home and sometimes also ventilate the home to improve air quality. They have a number of common parts and features used in most types of installations.

The *air return* with *filter* introduces external air into the system. It is drawn through a filter to remove dust and introduce fresh air. Exhaust outlets are the opposite feature; these expel stale air to allow fresh air to enter.

Heat pumps are becoming more popular as a modern clean energy source, with competing manufacturers bringing this ever-evolving technology to the market. Heat pump systems are best planned from the early stages of the build as they are not suited to late inclusion.

Heat pumps take heat from their surroundings, either external open air or from geothermal heat. Air heat pumps are simpler to install and these change air from the outside environ to create heating or cooling.

Ducts are smooth tubes acting as passageways for the air to flow freely. They do not work effectively if they are undersized or restricted and so the system is specially designed for each house. They will retain dust and should be cleaned every 2/5 years, dependent on the local conditions.

Thermostats are placed in linked zones or in a central part of the home. These are set to control ambient temperatures in the home by directing heat levels around the system.

Natural Ventilation.

The role played by ventilation is not always recognized in cooling systems. Rather than simply opening a window to ventilate a room, an air duct does the job by careful planning and design. Natural air-flow is directed by ducts taken through the structure and ducts expel hot air.

The benefits of this are immense. By natural means, you can cool your home for free, without mechanical power. Obviously, site-specific design must be considered and the direction of prevailing winds, etc. During colder periods, closing the vents allows heat to be retained.

Air Conditioning.

Heating, Ventilating and Air Conditioning (HVAC) is popular in warmer climates for home heating and cooling. As the name suggests, the system distributes heated air and cool air through ducts and this provides a pleasant environment inside the home in all temperatures. Some people are concerned by the apparent dryness of the air in the rooms but moisture levels can be boosted within the system itself at the design stage to reduce this side effect. The windows and doors of the home are normally closed during operation to avoid unintended additional warmer or cooler external air entering and upsetting the balanced temperature.

Criticisms of HVAC systems are sometimes raised because in older units, Chlorofluorocarbon (CFC) compounds may be released into the atmosphere, causing ozone depletion. Hydrochlorofluorocarbons (HCFCs), introduced in the 1990s, were weaker and reduced the damage but they still caused some damage. All new equipment should run on CFC-free and HCFC-free gas.

Forced Ducted Air Systems.

Forced Ducted Air Systems are popular in North America, Australia and New Zealand. Air is heated by a furnace and distributed around the home via ducts that are below the house frame or concrete slab. Floor grilles are strategically placed to provide heat across the rooms. Room thermostats and zoned areas can be set to save heating unoccupied rooms. There can be a form of air recycling; if installed, the air is then simply re-heated and re-distributed. A separate cooling system may be required.

Evaporative Cooling.

Evaporative cooling systems add cool air to your home by evaporating water. A cooling unit is fixed to the roof and draws in warm dry air. The air is filtered, which cools it down increasing its moisture content. It is mechanically distributed through ducts to the rooms and is released back into the external atmosphere through the natural ventilation of open windows and doors. This system uses less power in operation than HVAC but is not able to heat areas, only to cool them. In hot, dry climates, this system can be very effective but in more temperate areas a separate heating system is commonly installed .

Telephone/Cable TV/Internet Suppliers/Broadband/Digital Connection.

These services are all supplied by infrastructure companies and are generally provided from underground pipes into the house. The actual installation and routes are dependent on the current technology available in your area.

It can benefit you to plan ahead for these services. To assist the installers, you should run in a 2" (50mm) conduit, with a *draw line* running from your boundary to an outlet point within your property. Too often, this initial supply is overlooked and the only way to get a service installed involves an unsightly solution.

Wi-Fi Smart Home Technology (SHT).

These systems are best incorporated into the whole 'smart house package'. They can greatly improve the security of a home and give comfort to the occupants. The package can easily include security alarms, camera systems for remote viewing, remote door answering for deliveries, blind raising and lowering, swimming pool and spa operating, lighting activation and so on. SHT is fast evolving and many 'wow' moments occur when seeing a new development for the first time. They're finding solutions for problems previous generations did not even know existed.

Vacuum.

Built-in vacuum services were popular but are increasingly being replaced by individual, cordless vacuum cleaners (resting on charging docks) spaced around the home. A large single unit can have a very large motor and outlets run to convenient locations but they may not be as cost effective. Robotic cleaners are also a popular choice.

Chapter 8 – Action

- Decide which services you are to install
- Determine service ducts layouts
- Decide on a type of heating or cooling system
- Contact all the utility companies

CHAPTER 9
SUMMARY

Works below DPC set the tone for all that follows. Pinpoint accuracy counts because the services above, are connected to the services below.

Highlights covered in this chapter include:

- Foundation selection
- Soil tests
- DPM and slab penetrations
- All works under DPC level are very hard to fix later
- Drainage

CHAPTER 9

SITE WORKS – BELOW DAMP-PROOF COURSE (DPC)

'Progress is impossible without change, and those who cannot change their minds cannot change anything'.

– George Bernard Shaw

There is a natural divide between below-ground-level and above-ground-level works. Above ground works rely on the below ground structures for support, so both parts are equally important.

Works below ground exist in a damp location, from which the above ground works must be isolated in order to combat dampness rising from ground level. This requires planning, design and diligence. It is not so difficult to achieve, but you must be determined to get the construction detailing right first time. Changes second time round can be very disruptive. There will be crossover points where items and services rise through the levels, but you must be determined to seal off any pathway for moisture.

The dividing point between below and above structures is the damp-proof course (DPC). Below DPC level is formally known as substructure. This is the structure sub, or below, supporting the structure (the home) above.

The above ground structure is known as superstructure. The ground floor is included within this section as it is often used to protect the damp-proof course or damp-proof membranes (DPM) and these levels are more easily understood together.

Selecting Structural Foundations – What are the Common Options?

As part of the design process, all manner of questions will arise from designers over which construction methods are the most appropriate for your owner-build. The word 'appropriate' covers a full range; it can be ease of design or installation, based purely on cost or selected to meet local site conditions. It is important to have an overall understanding of all generally available options.

Structural Works.

These are the works which create the structure of the building. The integrity of the building and its very stability is dependent on the structure. All parts of the building are important and although the structure may not be visible after occupancy, it is fundamental and must be carefully managed.

Foundations.

Foundations are the lowest load bearing part of the structure and transmit the weight of the structure together with any imposed loads for windows, roofs, etc. into the ground. This plays a crucial part in the design of the whole construction project. The stability of the structure is totally dependent on the foundations. An engineer will always design a foundation for your home and in doing so, consider your above-ground design and site conditions. The engineer also considers the structures adjacent to your property and carefully designs your foundations so that they are not affected or de-stabilized.

A geotechnical or soil engineer at the direction of the structural engineer, attends site and take soil samples. They prepare a report for the engineer, who references their findings to assist with the design.

Purpose of a soil investigation:

- Determine the suitability of the design on this site given the ground conditions
- Give information to design an economical foundation

- Investigate changes in sub-soil conditions
- Highlight potential difficulties in the underground strata levels in order to influence design decisions
- Check if toxic wastes are detected

Only after this investigation can the design for your specific property be fixed. There are common foundation types often selected for residential buildings and it is always good to run through the various suitable options with your engineer.

Before any digging or earth moving, it is crucial you consider the probable positions of any and all services. You will also need to keep a careful watch for unexpected services and pipe locations.

All topsoil is removed before excavating for foundations. All organic matter, including loose timber, vegetable matter and roots should be removed and the area taken down to a firm base.

Toxic Contamination.

If toxic soils are found, they must be managed. The engineer will advise you on your specific site circumstance. A suitably qualified and experienced consultant may then be required to advise on a plan of action. Usually, contaminated soils must be removed carefully and dumped in approved sites. This can be expensive and so specific costs should be sought. Workers should be protected with site overalls and gloves. In almost all cases where toxins are found, the excavated levels can be built over after a layer of protection is placed across the site. All the structure and backfilling takes place above this layer.

TRUE STORY

A $6.7 Billion dollar project was stopped for over a year due to the absence of a plan to deal with the amount of contaminated soil dug out under old industrial areas. The initial contract indicated a figure of 5 percent of the waste was toxic but this was a vast understatement! Especially as the same employer, the state, had in the meantime changed the definition of contaminates in soils. They had not realised or even considered if the existing land-fill sites in the state could accept soil with this 'newly' given definition of toxicity. None of the sites within the state were registered to accept this soil. All the brainpower that a 6.7 billion-dollar project would employ should

> have realised that industrial areas are likely to have considerable amounts of toxic waste. This soil needed to be taken off site for safe and expensive dumping.
>
> You are facing similar challenges, just the scale is different. This lack of planning cost real money and livelihoods. It's worth learning the expensive lesson from their poor forecasting.

Concrete.

The common material in all modern foundations is concrete. Wet concrete is a malleable material that can be molded into any shape, and with steel reinforcement bars becomes an excellent material under compression. Your engineer will specify the concrete mix of aggregates, cement, sand and additives. It may be that different locations on your project have different specified mixes. The engineer will also specify a *slump*. This is a simple test that indicates the consistency of fresh concrete. Slumps are usually specified between 2"- 4" (50–90mm).

The batching or mixing of the concrete is usually controlled by the concrete supplier, so pass on the correct specification to them.

Vibration.

All concrete in foundations, columns and walls must be vibrated with a mechanical vibrator to ensure there are no voids under the surface and to remove air pockets. This will reduce honeycombing and increase strength.

Insulation must be fitted to all ground floor slabs to meet local energy-saving requirements. Expensive energy can be wasted through concrete slabs and consequently insulation is a valuable money-saving tool. Even in areas where insulation is not a building control requirement, insulation can continue to reduce heat loss and subsequent fuel wastage over the life of the home.

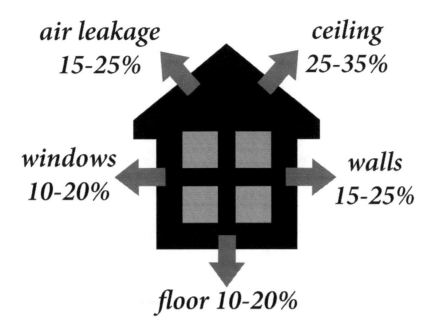

Heat Escape through the structure

Concrete Testing.

Your structural engineer can advise on concrete testing. Testing is set out at predetermined points; often each batch of concrete (each individual ready-mix truck load) may need to have samples taken and test cubes cast. These are collected from site regularly by testing laboratories. After 7 and 28 days, samples are crushed to determine strength. The concrete design will state what crushing loads must be achieved by each batch. It is crucial each test cube is faithfully recorded so in the event of a failure, the area the concrete sample was taken from can be identified within the structure. The engineer must see the results' test sheets to confirm all is well and should be copied in as a matter of course. Evidence of these tests may also be needed as part of your information flow to the building inspector. Look out for information on how to prepare cubes to achieve consistency. You should discuss the types of molds and numbers of cubes to be made as concrete samples with your engineer. Each test cube needs to be methodically prepared so like for like consistency of test can be achieved. Consider making someone responsible for sample taking and quality control.

Termite/Pest Protection.

Depending on your geographical location, you may need to include termite/pest protection to your foundations. In some areas, the building control inspector will require certification of the pesticide installation and so you need to employ an approved specialist contractor. Never spray before a rain shower as the chemical will run off and negate protection.

Movement Joints/Expansion Joints.

The engineer may specify vertical movement joints (aka control relief joints) and their location as part of the design. These are needed as the soil can settle under the weight of the structure and foundation by slightly differing amounts. Movement joints are introduced so walls and foundations can settle within designed limits without the structure cracking. By introducing movement joints, you encourage the building to settle where it can be controlled, along the designed joints. Suitable filling materials may be specified or are left as a void or filled with mortar.

An expansion joint is similar but is filled with an expansion relief material, which has elastic properties such as rubber or plastic. It is used on walkways, brick walls and concrete walls. It is installed in position before the concrete/brick is placed.

Damp-Proof Membranes (DPM) and Slab Penetrations.

A ground-based concrete slab is in direct connection with the earth. As part of the building control process, a DPM must be in place to stop dampness rising from the earth through the slab to the floor surface. The membrane can be plastic sheets with a bituminous covering to make it moisture resistant. DPM can be cut with a blade and connections carefully lapped and taped to prevent moisture getting through at the joints. The designer will show this 'DPM' on his sections showing the slab and foundation. It is very important all these details are carefully followed, as retrofitting is awkward and by no means easy to achieve.

Sometimes, a penetration must be made through the DPM, but only where it is unavoidable. It is important for each of these penetrations to be seriously considered and properly installed. Care should be taken to seal the penetrations so that damp is not allowed through. Breakages and splits in the membrane can lead to damp inside the house. If you can redirect a service so it does not penetrate the DPM, so much the better.

Setting out the positions of the penetrations is crucial too, as after they are cast in position, they are literally 'set in stone'. If you want to move or adjust these pipes, you will disturb the DPM, which is something to avoid as moisture ingress is likely.

Common Foundation Types

The engineer will normally suggest a common foundation type as these are well tested and are widely understood. It's just a matter of which is the most suitable and cost effective for your project. Particular foundation methods are preferred in some regions and it's important the installer is clear on how best to follow the design.

Strip Foundations.

Strip foundations are trenches that are excavated and filled with steel reinforcement and wet concrete. The engineer's calculations are computed on the basis of the dead weight of the wall above, bearing on the foundation center-line. If the weight bears on the edge, the foundation may be insufficient to do its job. Excavate strip foundations of any internal walls or loadbearing partitions to the same depth as external wall strip foundations, unless otherwise designed.

It is important for the excavated base to be clean, dry, level and compact. If they become waterlogged due to rain or groundwater, it is important that they are drained/pumped and dry before concrete is placed. If the site has a natural slope, steps are commonly introduced to the foundation. The designed depth is always to be maintained. Steps allow you to reduce excavation and subsequent removal of spoil, which in turn reduces the amount of concrete required.

If trench bases are going to be exposed for more than a short period, a dry, lean mix of concrete can be placed to protect the bottom surfaces and ensure they are not covered with loose mud. This lean mix base can also be used as a clean base to fix steel reinforcing placed in the trenches to increase the strength of the concrete. It is important all reinforcing steel is installed in line with the design and is laid on a clean base. Inert spacers (concrete or plastic) can be purchased from the steel supplier to space the steel up from the base or between the steel bars or mesh so that the concrete can fully surround the steel.

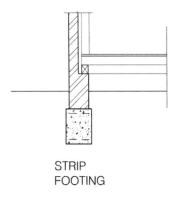

STRIP FOOTING

Raft Foundations.

This type of foundation is installed where the ground floor is to have a concrete slab. The overall site area is excavated, ensuring all loose or soft materials are removed. It is recommended, for working space, that a further 3' 0" (1m) perimeter is reduced all around. At the same time, all ground beams under the slab are to be excavated to the engineer's design.

It's good practice for the whole area to have a covering of *blinding*, a mix of weak concrete or granular material, which is compacted in layers not exceeding 9" (225mm). The structural steel mesh sheets and beams are installed in line with the engineer's bar bending schedules and drawings. The perimeter will be *shuttered* with ply and supported to contain the concrete.

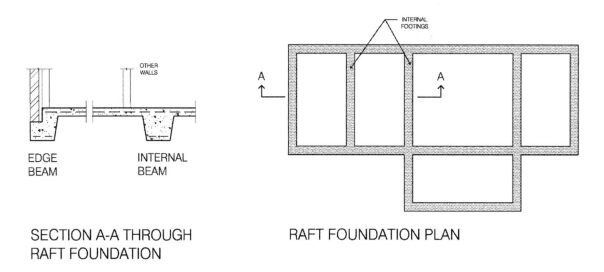

SECTION A-A THROUGH RAFT FOUNDATION

RAFT FOUNDATION PLAN

One of the great benefits of the raft foundation is exactly as the name implies. The slab acts as a raft over the soil and if the under-strata were to disappear in part, the raft would stay in position, 'floating' on the surface.

Slab Finishing.

Where a slab does not have a screed finish, it is smoothly finished with a power trowel or 'helicopter' specialist tools by the concrete contractor.

Piled Foundations.

Piled foundations support a slab sitting across a series of beams and piles. These resemble fingers of concrete bored into the ground, prepared to take bearing from deep solid strata. They can easily range between 6' 6" (2m) and 65' (20m) deep.

Piles receive support from the deeper, firmer ground if the shallower ground cannot offer the required bearing.

A specialist contractor, who may well have his own engineer as part of their team, will design their portion of the works, including installing the piles. Your consulting engineer will need to approve all designs and a testing methodology before any works commence.

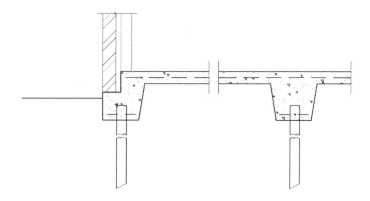

PILED FOUNDATION

The Piling Process.

The ground is cleared and the pile positions located and marked. The auger drills down to the designated depth and brings up spoil. This earth and rock is removed and reinforcement dropped into the voids or 'fingers' and concreted. Unless otherwise agreed, it is usually the owner-builder's responsibility to collect and remove this spoil. As with excavated soil removed to reduce the levels on site, this is subject to bulking. The piling contractor will ensure the placed concrete is vibrated and will usually be responsible for concrete cube testing. Test results will be provided to you on completion. The structural engineer will guide you on the required pile tests needed as part of building control compliance. The piling contractor departs with works complete at this point and the remaining works are the owner-builder's responsibility.

The steel in the piles is accessed by having the piles 'topped' at the height of the top of the ground beam. The contractor then excavates around the piles to the reduced level, which leaves concrete piles sitting up proud. The concrete up to the top of the pile is broken off, exposing the steel. The steel is then interlaced into the ground beams as per the engineer's design. This meshes the slabs and ground beams and allows support to be taken through the pile to the solid stratum below. This also connects the piles to the slab and makes them monolithic.

The ground beams and slabs are cast with *shuttering*. In domestic situations they are constructed of timber but they can be steel or heavy-duty plastic. This produces a slab with foundations bearing on solid stratum considerably below ground level. This is a very secure foundation which resists outside interference from tree roots or movement from other structures or developments.

Pad Foundations.

Pad foundations are isolated rectangular columns of concrete under the soil. They are laid out in a grid and act independently, bearing on the local soil. They are useful where a portal frame is specified, often as a structure for a swimming pool extension or larger independent garage. The concrete floor slab (or underground strips) tie them into each other.

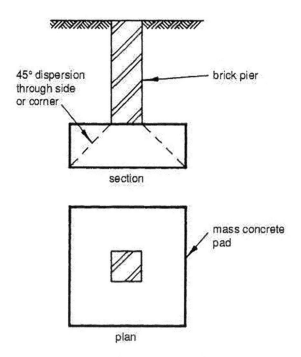

Section thru pad footing

Stump Foundations.

Stump foundations are mainly found in the southern hemisphere, although they are now less common in modern homes. They were often constructed with a series of timber posts, now usually in precast concrete.

So how do they work? Positioned across the floor area, stumps are individually set into the ground on concrete pads. Floor joists span between the stumps and are all linked together to provide a base for a floor covering. This was particularly good in warmer climates where a cooling breeze would ventilate the home from the underfloor. This type of ventilation goes against the modern trend of planned ventilation and sealed structures. Energy ratings are based on sealed and ventilated buildings so be aware of the issues before you select this floor type. Interestingly this design idea is having a revival with Passive House construction coming to the fore. A highly engineered steel post system is laid out with an off-site manufactured and densely-insulated cassette flooring system laid over. This is covered with tightly-fitted sheets that are sealed and airtight. This halts the escape of heat through the floor, one of the great energy loss points.

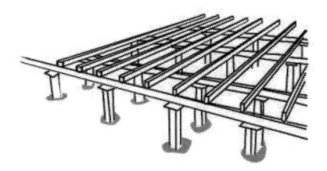

Stump footing layout

Screed.

The design can call for the DPM and insulation to be positioned on top of the structural concrete floor slab. In some areas, this is usual practice; in others it is looked on in disbelief. As long as you have a design and carefully follow it – local customs rule.

If this is the case, the finished floor level is laid as a screed. This is a sharp sand and cement mix which is levelled and spread. Two types of reinforcement are Polypropylene Fibers (PP fibers) and steel mesh.

PP Fibers.

PP fibers are added to the mix and assist the screed to manage stresses and reduce micro and large cracking that often occur. PP fibers also improve resistance to damage from impact or heavy surface abrasion.

Steel Mesh.

Reinforcement in screeds is often in the form of steel mesh, either specially manufactured high tensile wrapping reinforcement or a standard light gauge chicken wire. The sheets are laid covering the slab overlapping each other. The mix is laid over the whole area and levelled flat. This reinforcement will structurally strengthen the surface.

Screeds are commonly subject to surface cracking particularly around pipes where the cover thickness is reduced or through shrinking during the drying process. Screed reinforcements assist to reduce cracks but may not eliminate them. Plasterers or specialist operatives often carry out this work.

External Walls.

External walls are obviously continuous between below and above DPC level and are considered as part of this chapter.

External walls act as either supporting walls, taking loads from above, or are feature walls, for decorative, security or design purposes. They are usually solidly built, of various materials, some with high levels of integral insulation while others require insulation to be added either internally or externally.

The most common materials for wall construction are brick, timber frame, in-situ and precast concrete, aggregate blocks, SIP panels and compressed earth blocks & rammed earth. They may be clad to change their external appearance or left as the external finish. This may be determined by local planning requirements or by personal taste; as ever the important points are that it does its job of keeping weather out and warmth in all with a high quality of finish.

Walls in Foundations.

Strip foundations are sometimes designed to be poured to a low point and foundation walls are raised in brickwork and leveled to the top of the concrete slab. The external walls are supported by this brickwork. The walls below DPC level are allowed to remain damp but must not allow damp to rise either through or around the DPC. To achieve this, it is common for the bricks below DPC to be 'engineering bricks'. These bricks are of a higher strength than clay facing bricks and have a low water porosity. They are often left visible as a band around a house and the DPC is visible at more than 6" (150mm) above local ground levels.

Types of Bricks

Common Bricks.

Clay bricks are the most common type of brick, used to build external and internal walls. They are made in molds and so they are consistent in size and look. They can have a textured finished face or appear flat and smooth in appearance. They are often left as a finish or else covered by a cladding, render or plaster.

Sand Lime Bricks.

The brick color is determined by its mineral content and clay, with a high lime content producing a white or yellow appearance. When compared to clay bricks they are more uniform in color and are suitable in walls above DPC level.

Engineering Bricks.

Engineering or structural bricks have a low water absorption rate and a high compression strength. They are used in foundations below DPC, in manholes and retaining walls. They are more expensive than common bricks and are therefore best used where strength and low water absorption are important. Designers like to use them where the structure is on display and the brick columns are featured in their red or blue finish, supporting steel beams. They are also selected as coping bricks for walls for both their appearance and low water absorption rate.

Concrete Bricks aka Blocks.

Concrete blocks are available in many strengths and finishes. Some blocks are made to be heavy duty and designed for foundations as they have a low water absorption rate and a high loadbearing capacity. Others are lightweight and only suitable for internal non loadbearing situations. For 100 years, Autoclaved Aerated Concrete (AAC) blocks have been produced which incorporate inorganic materials and have air pockets that can give high levels of insulation. This all makes the material lighter to handle as well as cut and work with.

Pre-Cast/Manufactured Lintels.

Lintels are constructed as part of a wall to support loads above openings.

Concrete lintels are cast in molds as reinforced or pre-stressed reinforced. The pre-stressed lintels are where concrete is cast around high tensile stretched wires. This has the effect of allowing a 'thinner' lintel to be used to support a load that would otherwise require a larger reinforced concrete lintel.

Steel lintels are produced and they range from simple prime painted flat steels to 'L shaped right angle' steels & 'T' shaped steels that may be galvanized. The wide scope of products runs through to sophisticated insulated austenitic stainless steel with special finishes for aggressive and non-aggressive environments such as coastal and non-coastal sites. Lintels are designed for all types of brick and concrete block construction designs. The designers will guide and specify the most suitable products from this vast range.

Basements.

Basements can be constructed as part of the new home. These are more expensive to construct than upper floors as they require walls designed to laterally support retained earth. The foundations and walls will be designed by the engineer to mesh together and act in unison to take the loads imposed and keep out dampness. The walls will usually be either solid concrete blocks or blocks with voids that are filled with reinforced concrete. The option of solid, reinforced concrete walls cast in shutters can also be appropriate. Waterproofing concrete admixes are always of assistance in the battle against dampness.

Semi-Basements.

These rooms are partially below ground level. This can be useful where you wish to have an extra level or where height restrictions are a factor. As with a full basement, the room must retain earth and keep out dampness. The semi-basement reduces excavation and spoil removal and often results in slightly elevated living areas, which can have security and overlooking advantages. Garages are often constructed as semi-basements and are placed under the house, taking advantage of a natural site slope.

Retaining Walls.

These walls retain pressure, usually soil, and are included where the site is not naturally level and stepped levels are required. It is also common around the perimeter of the house, where the ground floor is dug into the site. By setting the walls back, retaining earth dampness problems are eliminated. Walls are often constructed of brick, concrete, and blocks that are core filled with reinforcement and poured concrete. A range of alternative finishes, such as timber and caged stones, are available. Retaining walls are not intended to hold back the water which can occur through hydrostatic pressure. It is important to design and install an appropriate drainage system, as without this the wall may structurally fail.

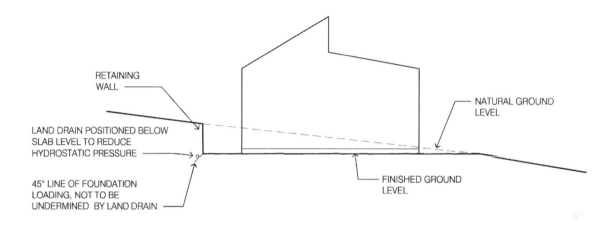

RETAINING WALL SET BACK FROM HOUSE

Vertical Damp-Proofing.

Where the design calls for house walls to structurally retain earth, there is a possibility of damp penetration, both vertically and horizontally. To meet building codes, the engineer will specify a DPM that is required.

All damp-proof work should be guaranteed in any case, as dampness is a difficult and expensive problem to eradicate after the works are complete. Insurance backed guarantees are generally available at an extra cost and are thoroughly worthwhile.

Drains

All homes must have a method of removing foul water and surface water from the property. This is taken to an outfall (usually a sewer) connection. There are very particular technical requirements for drainage installations and the selected material may not be your decision. Different regions have different requirements, with plastic and clay the most commonly specified material. Concrete and cast iron also have their places. All drains must be adequately supported and protected. The pipe material selected and the particulars of the installation will determine if the pipe is supported by concrete or shingle or surrounded in concrete or shingle. Some systems allow for flexibility at the joint locations and some for rigidity. Discuss the process with your designer to determine what the building inspector will like to see and approve.

If the infrastructure is in place, the foul water and surface water will be removed through a series of drainage pipes to a main public sewer and onwards for disposal. If not, you will need to deal with the waste in a planned manner.

The designer will include a drainage plan and the completed installation will be inspected & tested to confirm it meets the building codes before they can be covered by the structure or filled over externally.

If you do not have a main sewer connection to the property and the local public main sewer is available, then a connection to the main sewer can be organized through the state/province/regional utilities provider. If a sewer is not available, then you will need to install either a cesspool or a septic system. A 'Perc' or percolation test will establish how suited your sub ground site is to installing a septic or mini treatment sewer system.

Sewer Connections.

Private sewers are controlled by an individual or a group of neighbors, whereas a public sewer is owned and maintained by a public utilities provider. All connections to any private sewer other than your own must be by explicit consent. This permission should be recorded by deed to give your property enduring rights. Take legal advice on this point.

Design guidance on sewer connections will be in accordance with statutory requirements and state/province building codes. Normally only approved infrastructure contractors are allowed to connect to a 'live' sewer. You must check the specific requirements for material selection and installation and ensure compliance.

> **TIP BOX** Check to ensure *invert levels* allow for a suitable fall over the distance the drain is to run, from the highest point to the lowest point in your system.

Drainage and Treatment Systems.

Drainage must be compatible with local drainage installations and with the main sewerage system. There are three main drainage systems where the end connection is to a main sewer.

- A combined system, where all the foul water and surface/storm water are mixed and combine in the main sewer at a single sewer connection point. The mixed water is known as waste water.
- Separate systems for foul and surface/storm water; these are kept apart from each other and discharge at different fall-off points or separate sewers.
- Separate systems, where waste water is connected to the sewers and the surface water disposal is at a soak-away or water course.

If no sewer is available, what are your options?

Cesspool.

A cesspool is a tank which collects effluent. It is best located close to the house, but not too close! Access for removal of the effluent must be considered. The more you create, the more you have to remove.

Septic Tank.

A septic tank treats the effluent and requires a suitable local outfall, which may be a watercourse or ditch that is approved for this purpose. Many local governments are outlawing septic systems and require that existing systems move to full sewage treatment plants.

To provide some public health protection, both cesspools and septic tanks are required to have lockable lids. If you require either a cesspool or septic tank system, discuss this in detail with your designer.

Mini Treatment Plant.

A built-in treatment plant can be added if you have sufficient external space to treat and clean the waste on-site. With permission, this can be discharged into local watercourses. The key phrase is 'with permission'. Neighbors and local authorities can be cautious about self-treatment. Consultation is suggested/required.

Storm Water.

Storm water in our scenario is rainwater which collects into the drainage system. Flushing clean rainwater into the drainage system is not efficient and increases the liquid volumes entering the sewer system. It must not be filled into a cesspool or septic tank, as this water does not need cleaning, and paying for its removal by truck is an unnecessary extravagance.

Outfalls are required in some regions. These are placed within the site and the surface water runs into them. They also can be connected to ditches or water courses with permission.

You must ensure you connect to the correct system for your location. This means you may have to seek permission and probably have any connections carried out by approved contractors. This will not be a matter of choice; your drainage must comply with local practice. Additionally, as yours is joining a large local system, all properties must comply with local design practice as all the waste will mix. If the incorrect system is installed, localized pollution of the entire local system may occur.

The designer will allow for the following in your drainage design.

> **TIP BOX**
>
> Be careful with terminology.
>
> Often names are confused or used interchangeably. As well as using a term understand how the system referred to, operates. Mis-description or misunderstanding can be messy!

Capacity and Drain Runs.

The drain must be sized to ensure it can cope with the designed capacity. The number of persons or water-using machines, showers, etc. must be assumed and average usages assigned.

Your local water supplier will provide information on appropriately sizing your drains.

It is important to ensure all drains are correctly sized. Too large a drain will result in insufficient wash-through by liquids, leading to solids building up. Too small a drain may be overloaded and become ineffective. If you are connecting your drain to an existing run, then the users on the whole run must be taken into account. Your designer will consider local historical weather conditions to allow for unusual but not unheard-of storms and dry weather events.

Manhole Sizing.

Select manhole and access chambers by size as appropriate to the *invert* depth. Within the OH&S world, there is a movement for all manholes to be reassigned as access chambers. The idea is that they can be accessed, but not entered by, a person.

Connections run at an angle and turn in the direction of the flow. Pre-formed plastic manhole bases are popular and these predetermine the exit channels at suitable angles. Access chambers can be built from brick, although precast concrete and plastic are simpler to install.

Testing.

The drains are tested on completion, usually by a water test. This is a test where the pipes are filled by water to capacity and left in this condition for several hours. Water levels dropping or weeping joints indicate that the drains are not sealed. Air testing is preferred in some areas. The drains are pressurised and a pressure drop indicates a weep or leak.

The ground conditions will dictate the pipe material selected. It is often preferred to have flexible joints at the pipe connections as this allows the pipes to gently undulate in particular ground conditions. Again, your designer (and the building control regime) will factor this in before making a material selection.

Drainage Trenches.

The drain must run at a set fall to work effectively. If a trench is overcut, the gradient at the bottom can be raised with granular fill in order to set to the correct fall. Get the contractor to cut out any hard spots or rises to ensure stress points are removed. A stress point can damage the drain during its working lifetime. Remove soft spots and replace with granular fill. Leave 6" (150mm) each side for working room along the length of the trench. Carefully place bedding for support, ensuring your works do not damage the pipe. The drain must be covered on completion, for protection. Tamp the selected backfill to the pipes by hand for the first 18" (450mm). After this point, mechanical tamping can take place. Where rigid drains are encased in concrete, movement joints of flexible inert board are to be introduced at every connection point and at not greater than 16' (5m) intervals.

Distance Between Manholes.

The distance between manholes varies, dependent on drain size. This distance is set by your designer. Tables are published for each standard pipe diameter. A common interpretation sets the maximum distances between manholes at 330' (100m). This means each access chamber is not more than 165' (50m) from any point on the run.

Drainage Protection.

Drains must be protected from damage due to external elements. Damage can occur when drains are located too close to foundations, as these often transfer loads. Therefore, where a drain goes through a foundation, design consideration must be given to drain protection. Place a flexible connection at the 6" (150mm) point and the 30" (750mm) point of the pipes on both sides of the foundation. These are called 'rockers'. A similar solution is used through walls, with a lintel supporting the wall opening. Where the drain is excavated for and installed within 39" (1m) of a foundation, the drain will normally be surrounded by concrete and have expansion board placed beside the flexible pipe joints.

Issues also occur from above-ground traffic and below-ground tree roots. Combinations of these can also occur. Where it is deemed possible, take special precautions to protect the drains from damage. Manhole and access covers, frames and gullies should be of a type suitable to take the likely traffic conditions. Consider if they will be passed over by pedestrians or vehicles and get the appropriate items installed.

Ground Conditions.

If the ground water level is found to be high or the ground contains sulphates that may attack concrete or masonry, then special allowances must be made within the design process. The engineer will advise on this if issues arise from the ground report.

Sustainable Urban Drainage System (SUDS).

Surface water is good for ground soil, as moisture prevents shrinkage. If natural water is drained away, the ground can become dry and this can cause tree roots to extend to seek moisture. This can damage drains and building foundations. Dry soils can create foundation failure through 'ground heave'.

Part of the solution may be a sustainable urban drainage system (SUDS). This can be a low tech and inexpensive method of draining surface water. The system saves water from being wasted through needlessly running clean water into the sewer system. The idea is to have the surface water soak into the earth, maintaining a natural water level and so stopping flooding into water courses or streets.

This is often achieved by installing permeable paving, which directs rainwater on the surface of the paving block between the joints and into the earth below. It can also be achieved by slot surface drainage channels: taking water from driveways or hardstanding areas and draining the recovered rainwater into green, soft landscaped areas. Slot drains are available as precast lengths of channel with either a slot on the top surface or a removable grating. This retains the water in the soil, where it does the most good, and saves it from entering the drainage system.

Flooding.

The opposite problem to dry soils are floods and excessive surface water. National and regional flood authorities usually require that planning permissions include flood restriction conditions. Building codes have clear and ongoing directives to prevent water-saturated soils occurring within the lifetime of the development. Your design levels are commonly set to ensure the drainage system can cope with a 1 in 30-year rainfall event. With global change, states and provinces want to know that flooding will not damage infrastructure and are increasingly looking for protection against a 1 in 100-year climate change event. This is something to discuss with your designers.

French Drains.

A French drain system is a perforated drain encased in shingle. This system allows water to enter the drain from the external face of the pipe. It can also be sleeved in a geotextile membrane to stop aggregates entering the system. It is normally installed behind retaining walls to reduce water pressure on the structure, mainly in areas prone to flash flooding or surface water.

Land/Field Drains.

The land drain can be the same product as a French drain but is used to drain open areas of gardens or fields. Typically, land drains divert the water to a ditch or natural watercourse or to an approved drainage system. The fall on a land drain is commonly 1:50. The terms Land/Field/French drains are sometimes used interchangeably as they use a similar system to relieve hydrostatic pressure or reduce surface water and flooding.

Pumped Systems.

Where a gravity system cannot be installed, as the invert level is above the drain, pumps can push the effluent up to the sewer point. Pumps are located at the lowest point of the system, in sumps specially formed. It is advisable to consider a two-pump system so that a backup pump is on standby. Regular planned maintenance is advised. Include suitable equipment housing and an audible or flashing light alarm to indicate malfunction.

The works outlined in this chapter, in Chapter 5 'Starting Works' and Chapter 7 'Excavations' are known collectively as 'groundworks'. These are dirty and difficult but they must be mastered. It is often remarked that 'money is either made or lost in the ground' and you will come to realise the truth in this. These works will not be appreciated as perhaps the finish items will be, but make no mistake they are as important.

Chapter 9 – Action

- Discuss design with your engineer
- Confirm concrete test regime
- Confirm drainage layout
- Supervise ground works

CHAPTER 10
SUMMARY

The above-ground structure is what keeps the elements out and you safe inside.

Highlights covered in this chapter include:

- Floor and internal wall selection matters
- Window and door options
- Roof selection, roof drainage, and green features
- Planned ventilation

CHAPTER 10

WORKS ABOVE DAMP-PROOF COURSE (DPC)

'Life is like riding a bicycle. To keep your balance, you must keep moving'.
– Albert Einstein

Elements above DPC level are termed, the superstructure, they are supported by the substructure. The DPC level is the dividing and separation point between the substructure and the superstructure.

This chapter deals with the internal and external structure of the home and the coverings protecting it from external elements. This includes floors, columns, walls, windows, doors and roofs.

All are important in themselves but care must be taken connecting them together and protecting all their junction points. Buildings tend to fail at the junctions, not at the center. These are between all the points listed above and all joints, wherever they are.

Floors

Floors are specified by the designer/engineer to meet specific functions. They can be made out of many materials but fall into two general categories: solid and lightweight.

Ground Floors.

The selection of the ground floor as regards materials and design is largely a follow-on from the selected foundation. Many houses are constructed with a ground floor of poured concrete and an upper floor constructed from timber joists. This can be an efficient model, as the ground sub-strata takes the loading of the concrete and the lighter timber structure is supported by the ground floor walls.

Below are the most popular flooring selections in domestic situations:

Concrete Floors.

Insitu (cast on site) concrete floors are flexible in nature and can be successfully installed in new buildings. They are commonly designed to cover both strip & piled foundations and the floor is an intrinsic part of the raft slab.

All vegetation must be removed and the reduced level taken to firm ground. Only clean and appropriate granular infill can be used and it must be compacted in layers not exceeding 9" (225mm). If the total fill exceeds a depth of 36" (900mm), consider a suspended slab. Insulation must be laid under the area of the entire slab and care must be taken to ensure the integrity of the joints as heat can escape through any gaps.

Your engineer will provide a specification and the floor can be cast as a single monolithic slab or a structural slab with a screed top finish. Steel reinforcement (Rebar) is included within the structure to reduce the thickness but increase the strength. Concrete slabs are to be protected from being too hot or too cold. In heat slabs are covered for protection from the sun as drying out too fast leads to cracking. In the cold weather, the slabs are protected to avoid freezing as this can lead to cracking. Concrete prefers dry, temperate weather conditions that allow the concrete to cure steadily.

Precast Floors.

Concrete precast floor slabs are a popular choice as they are cast away from site and delivered only needing to be placed in position by crane. These are factory cast, often with high tensile reinforcement bars, and once on site are placed on top of supporting walls. Your team need not wait for good weather as they are manufactured to measurements and so fit straight onto the awaiting supports.

This makes them straightforward to install. The floor can be lowered onto brick walls sitting on a strip foundation.

For aesthetic purposes, the external skin can be raised above the internal thickness of the wall. With the 'inner' thick wall supporting the floor, the external skin masks the floor edge.

The precast slabs are also available with a high level of insulation fitted integrally. The insulation combats thermal bridging, reducing heat loss through the floor. Once in place with the joints grouted, the perimeter walls can commence within 24 hours. The floor is at its full structural capacity after 72 hours.

Block and Beam Floors.

A similar type of product to the precast slab is a block and beam floor. The supporting walls are similar to the precast floor system and precast concrete rails are laid on top of the walls. Concrete blocks are laid face down between the rails, ready to walk on. This is a low tech but effective and speedy method of delivering a structurally sound floor. A concrete topping/screed is then laid over the blocks. It can be worked on top of carefully the next day and will have increased significantly in strength in seven days. The advantage of this 'precast' floor is that a crane is not required, although some like to let machines take the strain.

Timber Floors.

Structural timber floors are a popular choice for ground floors. What follows is the usual process. Strip foundations are poured and perimeter and cross-walls are constructed. Bricks are laid, forming a solid wall and timber sills are set around the perimeter. Timber framing, made up of joists, span the cross-walls.

A solid *sub floor* is laid over the joists. This can be made of tongue and groove boards (T&G) or increasingly more likely is waterproof orientated strand board (OSB). The wall framing is taken from this subframe. Underside cross-ventilation is needed so as to avoid fungus growth and rot. The space formed under the joists can be useful and a good solution where ducted heating or HVAC is to be run in an underfloor void. Pipes and wires can be drilled through joists but must not take away the strength of the joist.

Steel Flooring Systems.

Flooring systems can have an economic advantage over the more traditional concrete foundations. They consist of a system of posts set into or fixed onto isolated concrete piers. This system was originally developed using timber posts but now galvanized steel systems are increasingly popular. The pre-galvanized, square hollow sections (SHS) can be MIG welded and a frame of steel joists fixed to create a ground floor level. A steel frame of walls and roof is supported off the base. This system is suitable on both flat and sloping blocks.

TRUE STORY

We were constructing a five-level commercial building, made up of two separate structures next to each other. On completion they joined together and looked like a single building. One structure was a steel frame for large, open office areas. The second was designed as a row of separate offices and built with concrete block walls and reinforced concrete slabs. It was a case of a modern steel frame adjacent to a traditional laid brick and concrete building.

Two teams started at the ground floor level on the same day and both work crews were up for the challenge of who would would reach the roof the roof first. The smart money was on the steel frame crew, as they had pre-fabricated girders to place and bolt together while the bricklayers and concreters had to build everything from blocks and pour concrete. It was not straightforward; the bricklayers and concreters had their materials and were self-sufficient while the steel guys were always waiting for something. The crane could only lift one steel girder into position at a time; a separate crew who laid the galvanized steel decking had to come to site, as did another crew, to weld the shear studs before the steel fixers could progress.

All in all, the build finish was a fine margin, taken as a tie. The moral is, modern methods may seem speedier but an organized traditional build can make rapid progress. On a single house, organization wins over any particular build system.

Upper Floors.

Upper floors are commonly constructed of timber joists. They are usually supported by a combination of solid load-bearing walls below and structural steel beams. Usually, only large homes with an open plan floor area would consider a steel structure and upper concrete floors.

Where an upper floor is designed as in-situ concrete, the floors are shuttered, with a timber deck held aloft by a series of adjustable steel props. Reinforcement is fixed to spacers to raise the steel from the deck so that concrete can surround the steel. Wet concrete is pumped to form the floor. The engineer will design every stage of this process.

U-Values & R-Values.

U-value is a rate of heat transfer through a material or structure from inside to outside. The unit of measurement is expressed as Btu/h.ft^2.F (W/M^{2}K). Building regulations require you meet or exceed specific U-values for various elements of construction, to limit heat loss from the building. The lower the U-value, the lower the loss. So lower is better.

R–Value is a measure of how well a material resists heat conduction. An R-Value is given for a window, screen or material and shows how well the 'thing' resists heat transfer from a warm surface (internal) to a colder surface (external). The higher the rating, the better.

Walls

Internal Walls.

Internal walls fall into two categories, loadbearing and non-loadbearing.

Loadbearing walls are designed to take weight and pass on weight to the foundations and so are made of strong solid materials. Non-loadbearing walls divide spaces and are often constructed of steel stud, timber stud or a type of blockwork but they are generally a 'lighter' form of construction.

Steel Stud.

Manufacturers have systems designed to meet a wide range of uses. Steel stud wall systems can be built up to 26' (8m) height and 12" (300mm) thick and are designed to meet fire ratings of up to 120 minutes. They can be designed to impressive levels of sound reduction.

Steel studs are light to carry and can be joined up easily by using tin snips to cut lengths and screws. They can also have services installed within their structure. They are finished with sheets of drywall.

> **TIP BOX**
>
> I have heard of complaints over creaking when steel stud walls heat or cool and thus expand or contract. By carefully following manufacturers' guidelines and correctly installing fixing brackets and connections, this phenomenon can be avoided.

Timber Stud.

Timber stud walls are effective and lightweight. The timber sizes usually purchased are 4" x 2" (100 x 50mm). The timbers are often regularized by timber planers to improve the surface quality and this can reduce their actual sizes marginally all around. Wood is a very good natural insulator and is well suited to owner-build construction.

Aerated/Lightweight Solid Concrete Blockwork.

Blockwork can work particularly well on ground floors with solid concrete slabs. Blocks provide a little more stability and are good where items require lateral or hanging support. They are often built where the area may be robustly used. Services need to be surface fixed or chased, as blocks do not have a cavity space.

> **TIP BOX**
>
> Single brick walls 4" (102.5mm) thick are not considered weather-proof. For economy, garages or outhouses are sometimes constructed with a single brick wall and this would need to be lined to hold back inclement weather. Best avoided as the cure is worse than the disease.

Wildfires.

Some areas require wildfire assessments and so each window and external door is given a fire rating it must achieve. Even if it is not a requirement, it is very worthwhile to conduct a Wildfire Hazard and Risk Assessment. It is a good starting point to work through the construction requirements to improve protection of the building elements against wildfire.

According to Proceedings of the National Academy of Sciences of the United States of America (PNSA), one third of all houses constructed since 1990 have been built close to vegetation, posing risks of combustion through the outbreak of wildfires.

The four most vulnerable areas of the home to wildfire attack are according to Firewise US:

- Roof and gutters
- Exterior walls including windows and doors
- External decking
- Near house landscaping

If passive features can be built in to help protect the house and improve performance by just being there, then seriously consider adopting these measures. Active fire suppression features such as sprinklers are worthwhile but preferably, they would be remotely operable. There are times when you need to be well away from a wildfire!

Research by Headwater Economics in the US has found new home construction designed to meet 'Wildfire Resistant' standards is only marginally more expensive. Careful substitution to fire resistant alternatives increased overall costs by approximately 2 percent. My view is that this small increase is more easily achieved if fire resistance is included as a central part of the design from the beginning. It is invariably more expensive to add or change features than it is to have them as part of the proposal. This is a sum well worth the investment. Indeed, they found that future buyers are keen on these features and reported that fire resistant homes increased by a premium of 10 percent over the equivalent standard home.

External Windows and Doors.

External windows and doors are an important part of the 'look' of any building and also a core functional point for the ambience and living experience. Windows are usually manufactured off site and delivered complete, ready for fitting. The materials most used for windows and doors are timber, aluminum, steel, PVCu (Polyvinyl Chloride un-plasticised) aka uPVC.

Each of these materials has benefits and any of them can be the most appropriate. Select materials based on the location and requirements of your build.

Front entrance doors are often manufactured out of wood, regardless of the material of secondary doors and windows. This is in order to make a design statement. Manufacturers also provide steel and PVCu 'wooden lookalike' doors to add extra security and provide multi-locking options.

Your designer will number the openings and normally produce an external windows and doors schedule. This schedule will show an elevation of each item and indicate ventilation and openings.

The selection of certain windows and door styles may be a local planning requirement in some specified zones, e.g. rural zoned. This can be due to local conservation area requirements insisting you match a local color or style. It can also be a safety issue, where local safety standards are set to keep property and people safe in the case of extreme weather conditions or natural disasters. Your designer will give initial advice if either of these issues arise.

It is usual to have set thermal values to match or exceed building control requirements. This gives you some tolerance over detailed designs and sets a standard you must meet.

You may wish to improve on the minimum required *U-value* and upgrade to a higher level, for better insulation. Where once double glazing was seen as the upcoming improved feature, triple glazing is becoming more common. U-values are also improved by exchanging the air in the cavities between the glazed panels with either Argon, Xenon or Krypton Gas, as these have a lower thermal conductivity than air. This reduces heat loss through the glass panes. The glazed unit manufacturers install the gas as part of their works.

The glass selected for the windows is a further option to consider. Higher specification windows have higher engineered glass to meet certain conditions. Windows can be responsible for heat losses of 25 percent. It is important to address all potential points of heat loss.

Consider ventilation through opening sashes or trickle ventilation. Trickle vents are long manually-operated ventilators which are inserted into the window frame. They are made to be opened in order to provide passive ventilation into the room.

> **TIP BOX**
>
> *Right screw for the job*
>
> Ensure you are using the correct screw or nail for a particular job. Trades people might, in apparent ignorance, use say drywall screws to connect structural timber members. This is because they are easier to fix and 'a screw is a screw'. This is not true.
>
> If the screw used cannot take the load imposed then it may, after a short time, snap and cause structural issues. If you are not sure of the appropriate fixing for any structural item, make it your job to find out.

Window Materials

Timber Frame Windows.

Windows with timber are often marketed 'trade', 'premium', 'high performance' or suchlike. Many specifications are available, including single, double and triple glazing, etc. Invariably, higher specifications lead to increased prices over the basic window models, although a higher specification window will serve you better in the long run. It is important to check the minimum specification and U-value you are required by building regulations to meet because different locations have different levels. Timber frame windows can be made with environmentally sustainable wood through forest management.

PVCu.

PVC is shorthand for Polyvinyl Chloride and the u is shorthand for un-plasticised. This material is well suited to window and door manufacture as it is resistant to weather and is a tough, rigid material which maintains its shape.

Aluminum.

Aluminum windows are popular with designers as they can be manufactured using thinner sections of frame and style than other materials and can have insulation installed within the cavity. Aluminum is strong and is suited to sliding/folding doors as the thin sections emphasize the glass and not the frame.

Steel Windows.

Steel windows are often used where the finished look should fit in with local surrounds and where a thin section of frame is required. Steel windows are usually hot-dipped galvanized, which protects the steel from rusting. Polyester powder coating can be applied in the factory, which can greatly lengthen time between re-applying paint finishes.

Aluminum-Clad Timber Windows.

These are hybrid windows inasmuch as they are timber windows which are clad with aluminum. This combination is popular as it gives the 'feel' of wood internally and provides the resilience of aluminum externally. This is a low maintenance option and mixes the 'greenest' window (timber) with the worst performing window environmentally.

Environmental Window Comparison

Material	Lifespan	Recyclable	Green Values
Timber	20-80 years	Yes	Timber windows have the least environmental burden during production. Timber is the highest maintenance window commonly manufactured.

PVCu	25-30 years	Yes	PVCu exudes large amounts of poisonous pollutants through its manufacture and throughout its life cycle.
Aluminium	25-80 years	Yes	Dangerous pollutants and high energy consumption during manufacture.
Steel	40 + years	Yes	Most steel used will have recyclable content, although the production process requires a high embodied-energy content from the mining and manufacturing process.
Aluminum Clad Timber	25-80 years	Yes	Mix of wood and aluminium, so is less green than timber only, yet it reduces a high maintenance element (the more porous wood), which reduces environmental effects.

Curtain Walls.

Many modern designs are moving towards walls of glass, with more glass used as guard rails for balconies. In order to get the 'look', designers are bringing forward complex structural curtain wall designs and rainscreen claddings. This can be a very creative solution.

The benefit of these designs is, they are striking when viewed both externally and internally. They bring in high levels of light throughout the home and homeowners can feel linked to nature by opening up the external views of gardens or landscapes. Windows, doors and screens are moving hi-tech, with surface coatings, electrochromic glass acting as blinds, and automated opening and closing.

The benefits of curtain walling are many and they include:

Flexible designs and the ability to personalize external elevations to make them distinctive and unique. If you want a special home which stands out from others and yet melds into the landscape, this can be the way to go.

Off-site prefabrication means windows and screens are manufactured and painted to your specifications but in factory conditions. This means high levels of quality control and an engineered and high-quality product. They simply turn up and are installed.

Frames are designed to multi-task. They act as thermal barriers, with effective *R-values*. This keeps warmth in the building. The cold is stopped from entering by installing insulation within the frame cavities. On hot days, the frames and insulation can stop warmth entering the building. Cold (thermal) bridging can be designed out.

Direct angles of sunlight entering the building will vary with the seasons and times of the day. These variations must be embraced and 'designed in' or else you may find the atmosphere uncomfortable at certain times of the day. Translucent panels can be introduced as light screens or fitted to roof openings to produce a softer and diffused light.

Avoid Problems with Maintenance and Repair.

Maintenance can be planned from the outset. If the curtain wall needs maintenance or repair, this can be addressed as part of the initial design. I put this in a positive light because then if it is needed, you will have a plan.

If you do not consider this aspect, then, say, changing a shattered piece of glass could be an awkward and expensive item. To keep costs low, complicated access should always be avoided. Glass panels may need cranes to lift them into position, particularly in inaccessible areas.

As with all selections, you and your designers have to manage all the consequences arising from your choices. Be aware of the following possible downsides, and design out these issues:

Framing and structural glass can have issues with buckling as they can be too flexible or the loads they support too great. Designers are looking for thin frames or glass-to-glass joints as this is the whole visual point of glass. Glass must be allowed to move but not be overstressed.

The engineers will allow for all expected weather conditions during the building's life, which in some areas can include overheating and freezing, high winds, and lashing snow and rain. This leads to differences between designers, who are after an aesthetic feel, and engineers, who are worried about weather patterns that may occur at some future point in time.

Seals and joint weakness cause deterioration of the assembly structures. If water or moisture gets past the joints and seeps into the insulation, this can (in any combination) freeze, thaw, heat, rot and lead to condensation and mold. Seals and joints must be carefully considered and treated to ensure they do not fail. If air escapes from a controlled environment (inside) to uncontrolled (externally), what can you do? If you have to reseal the joints, how do you access them?

Failing to prevent glass stress issues can lead to spontaneous breakage of glass, which is where glazed panels seem to fail and crack without cause. There will be a reason, but you know it will not be a straightforward fix.

Window frames are manufactured off-site to great accuracy but if your structure is not absolutely *spot on,* will joints get squeezed? If the design calls for ¾" (20mm) joints and site conditions have joints varying between 1 1/4" (35mm) and 1/6" (5mm) this is only a ½" (15mm) tolerance either way, will this affect the seals to the panels? You must work within allowed tolerances and meet them to be covered by manufacturers' warranties in the early years. It is also the case that the joints will be holding out against the elements long after the warranty period has expired.

If water does enter the frame, how does it escape? If weather turns wild, what can be designed in to improve the outcome? The consequence of water entering can be assisted if a channel is designed into the frame as a back-up, so water has a place to drain away instead of building up in the frame and causing damage.

Glare and reflection can also cause issues. If screens inadvertently redirect sunlight onto neighboring buildings, they can affect neighbors by increasing the temperatures of their properties. Reflection can also damage planting and grass landscaped areas. This concern can only be tackled as part of the design, since very little can be done later without major works.

Bird screens or anti-reflective screens can be installed onto the glass to reduce the likelihood of them not seeing the window and colliding with the glass. It can be distressing to find birds stunned or injured from colliding with your glazed screen elevations.

Once you have decided to go for a curtain wall finish, the designer can produce drawings and details to be sent to curtain wall suppliers. Once a manufacturer/contractor is on board, their designers can liaise with yours and take decisions. When all is decided and signed off, manufacture can start. Deliveries are scheduled and operatives arrive to a pristine workplace and effortlessly fit the frames to a perfect structure.

Well, this is the plan. Windows are, for many professional builders, a perpetual pain. It is hard to be too early in engaging with window manufacturers who, to be fair to them, have to build 'special one offs' as part of their daily business. There are so many details to be designed and confirmed and until they are all in place, nothing will commence.

Many builders have found the 90/10 rule comes into play. It seems that 90 percent of the time during design and installation is taken up dealing with 10 percent of the product.

> **TIP BOX**
>
> ### *Unintended Consequences*
>
> Unintended consequences flow from modern designs. I say this with all humility, but you are more likely to have issues with high-tech designs than you are with traditional designs. This does not mean you should stop pushing the design envelope and experimenting. You can, through imaginative modelling, have a vibrant home. It's just that you are specifically designing and butting new technologies together, so you must believe your designers have ironed out all the difficulties and unforeseen issues. Cutting edge designers are introducing digital twin technology which is the creation of a virtual 'twin' of your home. This virtual building can be tested to check that its design will stand up to the rigors of the real world. It will also indicate how well the design should work to reduce energy consumption. This virtual design world is at the early stages but be aware of the concept of unintended consequences.

Glass

Low Emissivity Glass.

(Low-e) refers to an energy-efficient coating applied to the glass surface. The aim of the coating is to control the flow of heat and cold air. This also protects internal surfaces and fabrics from fading from long-term sunlight, yet does not affect the transmission of visible light.

Low-e coatings are manufactured in two different types. Passive low-e coatings are designed to let solar heat into a building to increase temperatures and reduce the need for other forms of heating. This is excellent for cooler climes. The opposite type, solar control low-e coatings restrict light and solar gain. This is excellent for warmer climes.

Low Iron Glass.

Low iron glass is sometimes used to increase the clarity of vision through a shop window or in fish tanks. The glass is made with low levels of iron which removes a 'natural' tint in more traditionally manufactured glass. This can still be effective in double glazed windows and a little more economic if it is only fitted to the external pane of each glazed unit.

Solar Heat Gain Coefficient (SHGC).

SHGC is expressed as a number from 0 to 1. The lower the number, the lower the heat gain. A 'good' rating is currently recognized as 0.25, although a high-performance triple-glazed window can reasonably meet a rating of 0.14. The idea is to shield out the heat in the summer and keep the home warm in cooler temperatures.

Safety Glass.

Safety glass has safety features incorporated through its design. It does not shatter and so is less dangerous than regular glass. It is often required where windows and doors are located in places where collision between people and glass is considered a higher risk. Many areas require safety glass to be fitted where it is within 32" (800mm) of a walkway. Types of safety glass include laminated glass, toughened glass and wired plate glass. Safety glass can also improve the sound insulation rating of the window.

Locks

Locks are a feature often selected with purpose-made windows. Not only must you consider color, finish and size, but also general security, which is determined by the quality of the lock.

Some insurance companies require key-operated locks to be fitted to every opening window. It can be useful to order all locks in the house to be operated by a single key, rather than each lock requiring a specific key.

Multi-point locks on external doors can also offer greater security, and mostly work through a lever handle fitting. I consider that it is good practice for all external doors to be openable from the inside *without* the use of an internal key. This is to avoid delay searching for a key to allow you to exit the building in the event of a fire or other emergency.

> **TIP BOX**
>
> Patio doors are often fitted with sliding or bi-folding doors. Carefully consider the quality of the sliding door gear aka 'hardware' as poor quality or under-sized door gear makes for a miserable experience each time the door is opened or closed. Take advice, as the cheapest products are not always the best value.

Chimneys

Chimneys are increasingly included as design features rather than for heating purposes. Woodburning stoves have straight, steel tubes as a flue but brick chimneys are more complex and care should be taken with the design of the draft. A fireplace opening is constructed to take away smoke and is not intended for room ventilation. Offsets are designed as part of the flues so that the air escape is restricted or slowed. Closers can be installed to close off the chimney when not in use. They are rarely 100 per cent effective and there will invariably be some level of through ventilation (air circulation or loss) which becomes heat loss when the room is heated. In high wind areas, cowls are placed at the chimney externally to reduce the draft of air escaping from internal to external. If you have a chimney, it may as well work properly when it is called upon.

Where a chimney penetrates a floor or roof, ensure the surrounding structures are well supported and waterproof. As with any penetration in the roof, a chimney is an opportunity for a roof leak at the cross-over of materials and flashings.

Roofs

The obvious purpose of a roof is to offer shelter inside the house. All roof coverings should be evaluated for cost, finish, stability and longevity.

Roofs can be constructed in many ways, but a key feature and purpose is to drain away any rain as soon as it lands, effectively and efficiently. It's good practice, where possible, to always drain water away from the house, not towards the house. Sloping roofs drain outwards into gutters and downspouts. The joints between the edge of the roof covering and the structure of the building are always a place of higher risk of water ingress. A modern, well-built and insulated roof will have a massive impact on energy saving. This is achieved through high levels of insulation keeping heat in or stopping heat from entering.

Penetrations.

Roofs often have penetrations or holes for elements such as roof drainage, aerials, skylights, ventilation pipes, etc. Each penetration must be considered individually and assessed for any alternative options. If they are to remain, penetrations are a point of risk for leaks and appropriate care must be taken.

Holding Down Straps.

Roof members are constructed to the designers'/engineer's program. They calculate issues such as: weight of the structure, positions of supporting walls and structural members, etc. The designers will also have incorporated holding down straps into their design to secure the roof to the walls and reduce the likelihood of damage from high winds. These straps must be fitted as specified.

Ventilation.

Roofs are best ventilated by design. There are a range of ventilators available for every standard type of roof. Roof ventilation is a discussion you should have with your designer, as not only is it critical for the roof structure, it is also something your building inspector will check. All roofs, flat as well as pitched, should be ventilated. If not, condensation can occur and encourage mold growth. If unventilated, the structure and insulation can rot. This can evidence itself with the appearance of damp patches on your ceilings and a loss of effective insulation.

You'll need to clarify the whole issue of eaves design and know the difference between soffits, fascias and bargeboards. These are all critical details and yet many tradesmen seem to differ when it comes to specific installation details. As with concrete slabs, these are details you'll need to specify and make clear the outcome you want. I usually hand the tradesperson a standard detail or have the designer enlarge a detail drawing that shows how the parts are to fit together. Particular attention is paid to the ventilators and how they will passively draw air through the roof space (above the insulation not below!)

> **TIP BOX**
>
> Example Ontario Building Code
>
> The unobstructed ventilation must not be less than 1/300 of the insulated area.
>
> Unless separately venting each pitched joist space – cross ventilation must be provided.
>
> Not less than 25% of ventilation must be provided at both top and bottom.
>
> This example is typical of different areas having their own locally based codes. It is important local requirements are understood by the builder and all is made clear by the designer on their details.

Pitched Roofs.

Pitched roofs are set so that rain falls away by gravity. The minimum angle of the roof is dependent on where you are geographically, along with the predicted weather conditions. It is generally, however, around 25 percent fall. The designers and engineer will allow for exceptional weather conditions as part of their design.

A decision on the selected roof covering needs to be made before the engineer can allow for the appropriate weight in her calculations.

Pitched roofs are often covered in slate, either natural or manufactured, clay tiles or pre-painted steel sheets. They can also be covered in natural metal materials, such as aluminum, steel, zinc, copper and lead. These materials are considered more expensive but are used for their finished look or because of planning requirements on listed buildings or conservation areas.

Dormer windows are often incorporated where the top floor of the house is directly under the main roof. These are often covered in a metal sheet material with *flashings* and *cappings* to seal the sides and small roof areas.

Structurally Insulated Panel (SIP) walls and roofs may be constructed off-site and delivered for erection or fixed together on-site from lengths of timber and structural steel beams. A 'green' solution they are lightweight and strong. SIPs have excellent thermal benefits, which give a high energy efficiency, and are designed to limit cold bridging and reduce air gaps.

Flat Roofs.

The flat roof may be shielded by an upstand parapet or the roof covering can fall into a gutter. A fall is usually between 1:40 to 1:80, to allow rain to effectively drain away. The falls are achieved by tapering the roof surface by timber furring pieces or sand and cement screeds.

Flat roof coverings often selected are asphalt, mineral felt and high-performance felts. These can be left as the finish or have reflective solar paint applied to protect the roof covering from sun damage. A layer of white stone may be another answer to reflect heat. Alternatively, tiles made from recycled rubbers or otherwise can allow foot passage over the roof area.

A relatively new covering for both pitched and flat roofs is liquid applied membranes, which form a seamless covering.

Green Roofs.

Green roofs are increasingly sought after by planners as a way of encouraging bio-diversity in urban areas. Though more expensive, they have become almost mainstream and are now well understood by roofing contractors. They are basically flat roofs covered by a high performance felt, topped with sedum or soil. A growing, green finish is seen from above.

Care needs to be taken over plant/grass finishes as sometimes it can grow in a patchy way and look a little distressed.

Parapets.

Parapet walls are often designed as part of the look of an extension flat roof. This is where the external walls of the building extend above roof level and the wall is topped with a coping. Rain landing on a roof falls to one end and a further gutter is dropped down in the roof covering to take the water to a single outlet point. The danger is, you are by this design almost breaking one of the golden rules of roofs – do not fall water towards the house. The design is falling water towards the rear wall.

Remember to be careful over the details. The flat roof gutter must fall from one end to the other and clearly direct the water to the outlet. The wall flashing should raise above the roof by at least 6" (150mm) at the lowest point and be installed straight across the top.

Parapets are usually capped with a coping stone. This is commonly a concrete precast coping but many different designs are featured in new homes. The important issue is, the coping does not allow a path for rainwater to access the wall. Consider the coping and parapet as a single entity and ensure the DPCs and upstands work together.

Puddles.

Any rises or puddles can become a weak spot on a flat roof. Puddles by definition are pools of water, with an edge where the local roof covering rises to surrounding levels. The puddle will retain water after the surrounding roof is dry, and in sunshine the edge will heat up differentially to the water-covered puddle. This differential in time will damage and split the roof covering, weakening it, and leak.

> **TIP BOX**
>
> Always extend the coping stone over the edges of the wall on both the back and front by 2" (50mm) or more. Only purchase a coping with a drip line on the underside of the stone. This detail has been forgotten by modern designers and many leaks and streaky wall finishes are visible, highlighting this error.

Gutters and Downspouts

Guttering and downspouts are often overlooked but play a vital role. Rain landing on the roof needs to be collected and removed away from the building. Guttering can be discrete or become a feature of the home. It is not usually appreciated just how much water a guttering system controls, and if left to its own devices, how much damage rain can cause.

How Much Fall on a Gutter?

A 'straight' gutter should have a small fall to help the water run off to the downspout.

A fall of 1/8" (3mm) per 36" (1m) length is recommended.

A diameter of 4" (100mm) is the most common size of gutter on homes. This selected size should be confirmed with your designer.

Commonly, guttering and downspouts are underplayed as a finish and are there just to do a job; almost camouflaged in plain sight. The downspouts will drop rainwater into the strategically positioned drainage points and take water away through the drainage system.

Guttering and downspouts are invariably made from the same materials, with matching finishes. They are commonly available in colored uPVC and factory painted aluminum. The aluminum can be seamless, run off from a specialist machine on site, or purchased in standard lengths and cut to size for fitting.

If you want to make a feature of guttering and downspouts, you can install copper, stainless steel or zinc. Cast iron is often used in heritage areas, where it is a planning requirement. Gutter covers or gutter brushes can be a worthwhile investment as they prevent blockages, usually by leaves.

When making a feature of the roof water discharge system, I have seen designers include a modern form of the ancient gargoyle. This is where a feature discharges rain directly off a roof; by its size and overhang, it shoots away from the building. Wind can blow water back and chains are fitted so the water runs down and away.

> ### TRUE STORY
>
> I often notice the rear of a neighbor's property, but not in a good way. A fitting on the downspout half-way down the wall is indeed gray, as are all other pipes, but it is a different 'gray'. Each manufacturer has their own 'gray' and when products are mixed, they do stand out! Additionally, the down pipe does not run at a true vertical fall.
>
> Be careful when you fit the drainage, as *gullies* installed a little way off-center to the vertical downspout can be visually magnified by the downspout veering off straight to meet the drain

Rainwater Harvesting.

Rainwater harvesting is collecting rainwater and reusing it for another purpose. Water is easiest collected from rain landing on the roof. After transfer into gutters and downspouts, it's stored in a garden rain barrel or sealed storage tank.

As awareness of global climate change takes hold and the wish to store and re-use natural resources becomes commonplace, rainwater harvesting offers a low-tech, high result solution.

As a free gift from nature, rainwater collection is an environmentally effective activity.

This unchlorinated, stored water is great for gardens and saves you money. You can use it as an unmetered resource to fill swimming pools, flush toilets and to clean clothes in washing machines. It is, as yet, a benefit untaxed by any world government.

Tanks can be placed in an external area or planned and built in as part of the house construction. A simple pump will distribute the water where you wish around the home. Your designer will be able to easily calculate the size of each roof area from her CAD system.

TIP BOX

How Much Water?

Find out your area's annual rainfall and you may be surprised at your rainwater collection potential.

US Imperial Example:

Rain collection formula – 1 inch of rain x each sq. foot of roof = 0.623 US gallons.

So, for each 1000 sq. feet of roof, 623 US gallons of water falls onto your roof.

Central Texas receives on average 32" of rain per year.

So, roof of 2000 sq. ft. x 0.623 x 32 = 39,872 US gallons of potentially harvested rainfall each year.

Canadian Metric Example:

Medicine Hat Alberta receives on average 329mm of rain per year.

So, roof of 140m^2 x 329 = 46,060 liters of potentially harvested rainfall each year.

TRUE STORY

During an air pressure test, the results recorded were very poor. This surprised the builder as he had made great efforts to seal all the openings during the build process. There was obviously a problem, but where was it?

It was discovered that a plumber had made a hole in the external structure and not understood the implication of heat loss and insulation failure. This hidden spot was behind a bath and was simply not visible without close inspection. Air will escape, regardless of the visibility of unexpected external openings. Good practice dictates weather seals should be properly installed to all external building fabrics and thus energy use reduced.

Was it the plumbers fault for cutting a hole and not sealing it or at least telling the builder? Or was it the builder's fault for not specifically informing all site operatives of the importance of insulation and not to leave unplanned openings?

Avoid These Late-Stage Failures

Air Test.

Some areas require an air test as part of the completion and building control process. This is carried out and certified by specialists who attend your property. Even if not a requirement, it can be ideal to have the check carried out. It will give you a result of how well your building is sealed and if unplanned heat will escape.

They can, through this test:

- Confirm the property complies with the standards
- Assist by identifying where leaks are situated if the test does not meet set standards
- Check the performance of the planned ventilation system

Air tightness failure tends to come from two sources:

- Leaks at the joints of the external fabric of the building
- Service pipe penetrations

Air leaks can be inexpensive to avoid by thoughtful construction although expensive to repair. As the compliance test can only be undertaken in the final phase, an air test failure can be stressful because it only comes to light after trades have left site. Many consultants now recommend an earlier test is also scheduled at lock up stage. This will pick up issues of air leakage through the structure before all the walls and ceilings are covered and difficult to access.

Leak Tracing.

Leaks often occur where more than a single person/trade is responsible for a section. Therefore, the overlapping points of two trades has to be carefully monitored. An example would be air entering through, say, a small gap in two external wall finishes or around a window or roof hatch.

As with roofs, service penetrations (holes where cables pass through) are a cause of concern and must be avoided where possible in the first instance. If they are unavoidable, install all openings in the structure and envelope with care and inspect on completion.

Leaks in the external cladding or by penetrations should be dealt with at the source of the air leak. Once the leak is inside the structure, air passages can take cold air all over the building and come out say behind electrical sockets, spotlights, etc. To seal each and every leak is a major task.

Drafts Versus Ventilation.

Drafts are unplanned and uncontrolled air currents, entering and escaping from a home. Ventilation is planned air currents, entering and exiting a home. Increasing insulation levels means that higher levels of energy, once lost, has to be replaced and paid for. Insulation installed to maintain heat retention is estimated to lose up to 66 percent efficiency through uncontrolled air currents.

Good ventilation provides for predetermined air change levels, to keep the house healthy as well as the inhabitants. The house can employ mechanical 'smart' ventilation or old-fashioned grilles and manually-operated 'trickle vents' providing natural ventilation. Part of the air test involves sealing every ventilator so that air can only escape through unplanned exits. People are often surprised how many unplanned gaps there are in a newly finished building.

Where air tests are not carried out, it is becoming common on completion of the works to test for gaps in the insulation in walls and roofs by using photography with infrared cameras. By turning up the heat internally, gaps in insulation become obvious externally when viewed through the lens.

Lock Up Stage.

The building stage of 'Lock Up' is the point at which the building becomes secure. It can be the stage that all the structural works are finally complete. The external walls, roof, doors and windows are installed and the building is secure.

> **TRUE STORY**
>
> A recent court case (Skadberg v Buschholz in Canada) held that lock up can be determined by whatever terms were agreed in the contract. If you do not specify what 'lock up' means when you enter a contract, the court can determine what it means for you and will take 'reasonable expectations'. This means that in some circumstances not all windows and doors need be fitted, etc. Contracts that are specific are always better. This is relevant if you agree a payment plan based on stages of works being complete, not the installation of specific elements. It may be that your lender has a different understanding of what 'lock up' means from a contractor's understanding or indeed your understanding and will not release funds. This can be awkward if your contractor is expecting an invoice to be paid. Always define what terms mean to avoid confusion.

Keys.

Security should be maintained during the remaining building process and also after completion. Key security should be a priority as lost keys necessitate substantial costs for replacement and also introduce unnecessary stress. Keys should be recorded and issued to individuals who are to take responsibility for their care and return.

Before lock up stage is a good time to decide on keys and access. A master key system can be incorporated so that you don't need multiple keys to open and lock up the house. A sophisticated keyed system can be applied where each door has a separate key, although a single master key will open all doors. Variations to choose from include fob systems, digital key pads, fingerprint or iris recognition access controls. The more sophisticated or technical the system the earlier it should be investigated.

Chapter 10 – Action

- Be aware of structural design choices as they impact on selected finishes
- Insulation is to be carefully installed and checked for missing spots
- Visit manufacturers and compare window styles and types
- Test and fix air leakage
- Design a water harvesting system
- Select a key security system

MONEY/TIME
Budget & Cash Flow
Finance Timings

DESIGN
Clarify Trade Crossovers
Amend As-built Drawings
Fit Out Selections

WORKS
Start To Complete Works
Check QA/QC

CHAPTER 11
SUMMARY

These are the works you and your visitors will see. They set the feeling of quality of the home.

Highlights covered in this chapter include:

- Equality of access and lifetime standards
- Stair design
- Plastering v Drywall
- Security

CHAPTER 11

FIT OUT

'Marriage is a long meal with desert served at the beginning'.
— Stanley Kubrick

(Is homebuilding similar?)

Fit out refers to all internal works after the structure and external weather protection is complete. Quality of workmanship at the fit-out stage is generally perceived to indicate the quality of the home. The finish is what you will be judged on. Of long-term importance, this is a chance to stamp your personality on the look and feel of your living and private areas.

All the fit-out choices matter. You must see them as a whole, with the finishes of areas and rooms all uniting the style and design. How you theme and dress your home will be crucial to how much style it projects. Good taste may not always cost more but it is always subjective.

As the fit-out stage is all about quality of finish, it's worthwhile visiting showrooms to see and touch potential materials and finishes before purchase. Things are not always as you expect… sometimes they are better!

Work through each room or area, much as you did at the program stage, and select finishes with an idea of the overall style of your dream home.

- *Are you having painted surfaces or wallpaper?*
- *Are you having panelled or flush (flat) doors?*
- *Are you having contrasting styles in any areas or rooms?*

Every area will throw up many different questions, all of which you need to answer.

Bring it All Together.

To assist your contractors, a schedule detailing the finishes for each area can be very useful. This will become the basis for a pricing document as it will clearly explain what finish is wanted where.

Consider how things will fit together and where items are be stored. Select the fitted cupboard doors and wardrobe doors. What finish will they have and will they match or complement?

Finish Schedule - Tiles

	Floor	M²	Wall	M²	Feature	Comments	Bath Panel	Skirting
B1 Ensuite	MAXMT 1000 Belgium Stone Bruno Lapparto 600x300	7m²	MAXFL1180 BELGIUM STONE ICE NATURAL Lapparto 600x300	10m²	None	The tap is wall fixed - cut hole in tile.	None	MAXMT 1000 Belgium Stone Bruno Lapparto 600x300
B2 Ensuite	MAXFL1037 Strato Nero Natural 600x300	6m²	MAXFL1028 Strato light Grey Natural 600x300	8m²	None	The Strato Nero Natural is not showing on the webpage as 600x300. If you can not get it, please get Stratos Nero in 600x300. Please get Lapparto finish if available. The Strato Light Grey Natural is not showing on the webpage as 600x300. If you can not get it, please get Stratos Light Grey in 600x300. Please get Lapparto finish if available.	As Floor	MAXFL1037 Strato Nero Natural 600x300

It can be nice to have a few little surprises in a new build. This will differentiate your house from others. This could comprise a secret door to a private room or office or a built-in appliance not normally included within the specifications by a house builder. A bonus of an owner-built home is that you are in charge and you do not have to provide a standard finish. It is your chance to shine.

Equality of Access.

The US and Canadian governments encourage all new homes to have equality of access for all. Canada has the concept of 'Flexhouse' and the US 'Universal Housing'. As the owner-builder, there is no reason that you cannot easily design your home as 'user friendly' to a person with a disability or wheelchair user. This can mean something as simple as widening a door to 36" (900mm) or having a level entrance at the front and rear door, a wider corridor or wider ground floor bathroom door. At a future point, the floor covering could be changed from carpet to laminate to be more wheelchair friendly and smart lights could allow mobile phone apps to switch lights on and off. Light switches and power points can be placed at accessible heights for wheelchair users.

These features will make alterations easier if your family circumstances change. Accessible design will allow residents to remain longer, rather than struggling with the access barriers encountered in many homes. If you are proposing to live on more than a single level, consider an elevator or leaving space so that one can easily be installed at a future time.

Drylining & Plastering.

Plastering and dry wall finishes are what you see of the walls when the works are complete. Unfortunately, given how much has been put into the building at every other stage, the perception of quality is taken from the finish. Small flaws are highlighted by paint and by sunlight coming into the house at different times of the day and season. All in all, having a high-quality wall finish will be one of the major factors in you feeling happy at the end of the build. A good job was done.

Drywall can be fixed to the room-side of external walls and to internal walls.

Many different types of drywall sheets are available on the market, offering features with benefits like fireproofing, asthma reducing, sound deadening and moisture and vapor resistance. Select the correct sheet to meet building control requirements and to fulfil the purpose of the room. Manufacturers do make moisture resistant boards but these are recommended for intermittent moisture applications in bathrooms etc. Adjacent to showers and baths, many choose to use a higher moisture resistant cement sheet as a backing board for tiles.

Drywall can be fitted to solid walls and stud walls by special adhesives commonly known as 'Glue' 'Dot and Dab' or 'Stick & Fix'. Some tradespeople like to 'Glue and Screw' which is covering all bases.

If external solid walls require upgrading to meet a U-value sought by local building codes, this can be achieved by surface fixing drywall internally with insulation glued to the rear surface.

Lightweight walls are usually covered with drywall and secured or 'tacked' by nails or drywall screws through to the timber or steel stud structure.

> **TIP BOX**
>
> It can be worthwhile to add strengthening under the drywall sheets. This assists if you intend to hang cupboards or heavy pictures or if you just don't want to be concerned with fitting secure fixings. A layer of ¾" (18mm) ply sheeting can be fixed to the surface of the studwork. This also has the effect of adding strength to the wall. Sheets can be fitted over the top, serving to sandwich the ply against the stud wall and the backside of the drywall. Fix the ceiling sheets first and the walls second. As with everything start at the top!

Drywall comes in two edge finishes – square edge (butt edge) and 'V' (taper) edged. Square edge is installed where a skim 'wet plaster' finish is to be applied and 'V' edge where drylining (taping and jointing) is the finish.

It is common to first run services through wall partitions and any insulation is installed afterwards. The usual method is to affix the wall sheets to one side of the partitions and then run in the service lines. The second side is covered with securely fitted drywall. The surface of the sheet is sealed both sides with a finish and awaits decoration.

In general terms, for partitions, screws are located at 12" (300mm) centers 8" (200mm) centers at external angles. For ceiling systems, the screws are located at 9" (225mm) centers within the middle of the board and 6" (150mm) centers at board ends. However, these general guidelines may vary depending on the system used and so reference must be made to the manufacturers' information sheets.

A wide range of angle beads and spacer beads are available. These can reinforce external wall corners or divide larger wall surfaces into divided or defined sections. This can reduce drying out surface cracking or provide an attractive finish option to an otherwise largely bland wall.

Wet plaster is applied when a harder or water/splash resistant surface is needed. This can be applied to the internal surfaces of external walls and ceilings, or to solid or lightweight partitions. Each type of location (e.g. bathroom, kitchen) has a wet plaster best suited. Different materials and their applications are easily sourced through manufacturers' websites.

Stairs.

Stairs can be an opportunity for design statements which give the home a *wow* factor. The option of spiral stairs is often considered but most designers do not believe they save floor space and are usually only selected as a design decision. Stairs can be made extra wide for effect or have LED lighting built into the treads or risers for illumination or style. On this, natural light is always good, and if directed through light pipes or dome lights, can provide useful daylight.

From a design perspective, as a walkway the steps linking two levels should all be identical in height and *going*. The number of steps is calculated by measuring the height distance between the two levels and dividing this dimension by a reasonable step rise. Stairs can be steep or 'slow'; by being aware as you walk up and down flights of stairs, you will soon appreciate what this means.

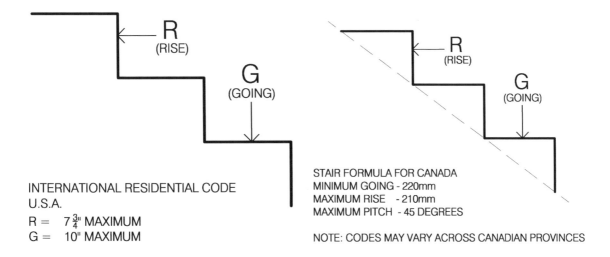

INTERNATIONAL RESIDENTIAL CODE
U.S.A.
R = 7¾" MAXIMUM
G = 10" MAXIMUM

STAIR FORMULA FOR CANADA
MINIMUM GOING - 220mm
MAXIMUM RISE - 210mm
MAXIMUM PITCH - 45 DEGREES

NOTE: CODES MAY VARY ACROSS CANADIAN PROVINCES

The maximum US riser height is given by the International Residential Code (IRC) as 7 3/4" (196mm) and the maximum going (tread) of 10" (254mm). The width of the stair is generally 36" (914mm) but is no less than 32" (812mm). Handrails are set between 34" (864mm) and 38" (965mm).

There are some state variables so confirm your local requirement.

The maximum Canadian riser height is given as 200mm (8") and the minimum going (tread) of 255mm (10"). The width of the stair shall not be less than 900 mm (36"). Handrails are set between 865mm (34") and 965mm (38").

There are some variables across the provinces so as ever check your local code.

External garden stairs are often built shallower with a lesser pitch and here the old imperial rhymed saying of '7 / 11' stands in good stead. This relates to a 7" (175mm) rise and an 11" (275mm) tread. Although often this is reduced / increased to 6 / 12. This means a 6" (150mm) rise and 12" (300mm) tread. Depending on the ground levels, you can also make a feature of the tread and have them up to say 39" (1m) or more.

The most common stair material is wood, although other materials can be used to great effect.

Timber stairs are made to standard sizes and sold by the large shed-building materials suppliers or can be made-to-measure off-site at a specialist workshop. Hardwood stairs can be purpose-made and become a stunning feature but the material is at least twice as costly, if not more. If the stairs are to be carpeted, then a softwood/MDF stair is sufficient.

Steel stairs offer slender finishes for the strings and risers and can themselves be highlighted to great effect. With dramatic lighting, they can act as a contrast to all the other material selections in the home. The functioning staircase thus doubles up as an illumination. Steel staircases are made and fitted by metal workers.

Concrete stairs can be cast in-situ or supplied pre-cast. Like steel, they offer an alternative and strong feel to the interiors. They are best going between concrete floors.

Doors.

Doors are purchased as standard finished items or as door blanks cut to fit a special size.

As with stairs, doors can be a major factor in giving a sense of style. By being taller and/or wider than usual, they may make an architectural design statement. They are generally purchased ready for painting or come with a veneer finish.

For effect, doors in some house styles work well when supported by a sliding door system. As well as a special feature, they can be a space-saving device. Sliding doors, if not surface mounted, can be fitted internally into the stud wall cavity by installing a cavity sliding system, hidden by the wallboard.

Always take advice on the quality of the system, as a sliding door continually binding or slipping off the track is very annoying for the user.

Floor Pivots & Hardware.

Recessed *floor pivots* can make a normal opening grand, particularly if the opening size is enlarged. Care has to be taken with external pivot front entrance doors, as they need a large gap to sweep open. This can lead to an unwanted draft!

Pivots can be specified to act as you want them to. They are sold as single opening or two-way opening, and if you would like either type to stay fixed open at 90 degrees, then you should also specify this feature as it will not be standard.

Hinges and locks are important and can be carefully selected after you have determined any requirements of building control. Discussion with tradespeople over number per door, style, gauge and position can be useful. Everyone seems to have an opinion, though yours is more important than anyone else's. Solid, heavier doors should have a minimum of three hinges and if a fire door, the number and spacing may be mandated by the building inspector.

Internally, doors and frames are fitted to walls for privacy or separation between rooms, and there are tricks to this too. The simple technique of setting out doorframes a little way from corners can avoid the sloppy mistakes of non-thinking construction, i.e. the doors being off center in the opening or too close to a wall or window.

The setting out of windows and doors may also be raised as a problem when they are positioned too close to each other. A little thought during the construction of the internal and external walls will prevent these problems.

Garage Doors.

Garage doors must obviously be wide enough to allow vehicles to pass through. That concern met, next you must consider the automatic door or another type. If you select an electrically-operated door, you must take careful advice over the motor size and lifting weights. A common mistake is to install a door too heavy for standard lifting gear. This is particularly the case where a special finish is applied to the frame of the door, to match some other part of the structure. A garage door contractor will be well versed in this and if they supply door and motor, all should be well.

TRUE STORY

> The local planning conservation inspector insisted a double garage door be made of timber. Our team did not consider the weight and we had the approved door (with glazed panels) purpose-made and delivered. The problem was buying a motor with enough power to lift the dead weight. After a lot of research, we did locate a beast large enough but it was a close call. Calculate the weight and design of the door and ensure the lifting gear can cope before you place an order!

Baseboard and Trim.

Baseboard and Trim are a part of the finish of any room and deserve respect they do not always receive. They are a visible feature, acting as a cover where materials cross-over that are likely to crack. Both are widely available in many finishes and moldings, from traditional 19th Century to the most modern take.

Regrettably, these elements are sometimes poorly installed, with gaps at their mitres, or not installed level. My special horror is doors with a molding on one side and top, with a quadrant (a quarter milled piece from a circular timber) down one side. This is often on the inside of a door; 'space' is cited as the excuse. In truth, this is usually a result of poor setting out and invariably this problem could have been solved by thinking ahead and measuring accurately. This should not be allowed to become an issue!

Hooks and Handles.

Work through the various rooms and think through coat hooks, handles, toilet roll holders, towel rails, etc. Once scheduled, the numbers of items involved can be surprising. Selection of these items is as important as any other and with a little planning, you can select matching fittings for all areas of the home. A schedule of items can assist the carpenter to put the right hook in the right room. It may be easier to go shopping with schedule in hand and purchase these items personally. This will give you an opportunity to feel the quality of items at the store. These can be issued to the operative or retained for self-fixing. If you are compiling a specification for a contractor these items can be noted as 'owner supply' and so only a fixing cost need be included.

Kitchens.

The kitchen is the central hub of many homes. They can be basic places to warm food or for elaborate gastro experiences. They may also be entertaining areas, where dining is common.

The big divide in the kitchen world is over the question of how cabinetry is sourced. Are they standard sized units, pre-made in a modular form, or are they units custom built after a careful measure of the finished walls. However, much of kitchen design is based on personal preference and what you have found works for you.

Your initial thoughts will be over travel distance between the sink and dishwasher, the sink and refrigerator, and so on. Try to avoid drawers opening onto other drawers so that one has to be closed before the other can be opened and allow spacers to offset corners. Look at where the refrigerator door might open. Then it's onto the exciting part: cabinets, benchtops, backsplash.

The selection of possible units is huge, but you need clear decision-making to design a good working kitchen.

One thing to be aware of is the 'standards' that have emerged concerning heights of worktops, base units and wall cabinets. These are not laid out as building codes but rather have become accepted norms. A look through a pre-made kitchen unit catalogue will soon confirm the standard dimensions. They are all basically the same dimensionally, with the worktop set at 36" (900mm) above the floor finish.

Unit widths range from 12" (300mm) to 48" (1200mm). Be careful of space within a kitchen and the dimensions needed to effectively work between units.

Worktops can be selected in timber, laminate plastic, stone or concrete finishes. The important issue is ensuring the worktop is impervious and hardwearing. The worktop can be a relatively inexpensive 'styling' point and can pick up the whole feel of the kitchen.

Templates.

Be wary of templates. Many granite, composite stone or concrete worktops are manufactured specially for your kitchen from handmade templates that are produced after the base units are fitted. They will make *whatever the template indicates*. It is safer to pay a little more for the supplier to visit site and produce their own templates. Then if there is a problem with fitting, you have someone to go to!

The kitchen is an important room to get right and an opportunity to set a standard and bring innovative design to new fittings and layout ideas. Listing and selecting your appliances will assist as you can include the actual dimensions of the appliances, and if required, design in ventilation spaces.

Wardrobes and Cupboards.

The wardrobe is a storage place for clothes and a whole lot more.

Wardrobes and cupboards can also bring more pleasure to living in the home. There are many clever hanging and storage systems, which can greatly impact how you live. Conversely, a common complaint of new houses is in regards to insufficient storage.

The storage element must reflect the amount of stuff you usually store in wardrobes and cupboards. Not enough storage leads to things becoming messy or stored in inappropriate places. This is code for 'irritating places'… but it is certainly not the purpose of the owner-built house to be irritated on a daily basis.

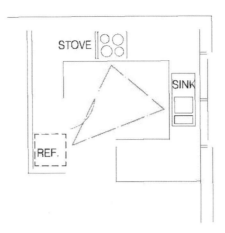

KITCHEN WORKING TRIANGLE

Whichever way you decide to go, the emphasis must be on layout and design. This is important and must be right. 'Nearly right' is annoying in the extreme, so take great effort to consult and ruminate on the final agreed design.

Bathrooms/Showers.

These are important and expensive rooms that affect your enjoyment of the home. A careful survey of your family likes and dislikes can be interesting. Decisions over bath-versus-shower and fixed shower head over showers on hoses (or a combination of both) can lead to people who did not know they felt strongly about this subject, quickly getting passionate.

Bathrooms (especially ensuites) may be small but still effective. *Wet rooms* have become popular, where the whole room is sealed and waterproofed. Specialist waterproof underlay trays are fitted to the floor and covered with an impervious tiled surface. Waterproofing allows the shower screen to be omitted or made unobtrusive and this can give the feeling of space rather than restriction. The obvious concern is leaking, so again, diligence with details is necessary.

Ventilation should be planned and the hot, moist air effectively removed. Otherwise, mold can appear on wall and ceiling surfaces.

Do you want to use the mirror straight after showering, but usually cannot see a thing? Heat pads can be fitted to the back side of a fitted mirror to keep the temperature up so that condensation is avoided on the mirror surface. This may seem a solution for a non-existent problem, but once you have one fitted, you will do so again.

PHILIP FITZPATRICK

Hard and Soft Floor Finishes

Floor finishes cover materials such as timber, ceramic tile, stone, concrete, rubber and woven carpet.

Timber Floors.

Solid timber floors can be purchased as square edged or tongue and groove (T&G). The prime advantage of solid boards is the ability to sand them multiple times and re-coat them to retain a pleasing finish. Many different woods are suited to flooring and they are exported all over the world. You may wish to consider using locally-grown wood, to reduce carbon miles of travel and is sourced from a renewable forest environment. The Forest Stewardship Council (FSC) labels should be attached to products sold that are registered to meet the FSC forest management standards. Each supplier will have a unique Chain of Custody certificate number that you can check is valid. The National Wood Flooring Association (NWFA) has a National Oak Flooring Manufacturers Association (NOFMA) certification scheme that confirms performance and quality levels of many types of hardwood flooring.

Laminate floorings are increasing in popularity and are manufactured through a synthetic multi-layered lamination process. The finished product looks like wood but is a wood image (photograph if you like) that is covered with a protective surface layer. It is popular as it is economic to purchase although it cannot be re-sanded and sealed if scratched. It is a cheaper finish that suits many a budget.

Engineered hardwood timber finished floorings are widely used. They look similar in finish to laminate boards but are crucially different. They comprise a solid particle board covered with a thin layer (laminate) of the solid finished wood.

The advantage of a combination of particle board and laminate is, it tends to be more stable than solid wood. Engineered flooring suits underfloor heating as the warmth created under the floor does not expand or warp the floor. This can happen with solid hardwood flooring.

Engineered board is thinner than solid wood and so the boards can only be sanded 2/3 times before totally removing the laminate finish. It is normal to sand and re-seal every 4/6 plus years, so you may have to think how long a period between floor replacement is appropriate for you.

Hybrid Rigid Core is a newer product that is vinyl but has the appearance of wood. It comes in a 100% waterproof finish and is good as a hardwearing surface that is pet friendly. It is not technically a wooden floor but it is competing within this market.

Wooden floor types can be purchased plain or finished with a matt or gloss lacquer. Floors are something to be considered as a cost point but also as a finish. A visit to a few showrooms should sort out the outstanding issues.

Ceramic & Porcelain Tiles.

The larger category of ceramic tiles divides into two types: porcelain and ceramic. They are close relatives but porcelain is more impervious to wear than ceramic, with a lower level of water penetration. Porcelain is considered to be denser, finer grained and smoother.

Ceramic tiles are easier to cut and only suited for indoor installation. They are generally the least costly option. Porcelain is harder, more durable and is often specified for bathrooms and swimming pools. The market range for both ceramic and porcelain is so large it can be confusing. Therefore, it's best to compare particular tiles to ensure they are suitable to be fixed in their designed location.

Quarry tiles are so called because the materials used to create them are quarried. They are extruded to retain their color throughout and can include a textured surface. They are suitable for both external and internal floors. Quarry tiles are nonporous as they are fired at very high temperatures. They are sometimes used for rain screen external cladding but in domestic situations this would be unusual, although they can be striking in hi-tech designs.

Glass Tiles are very good at being wiped clean but can chip along the edges. They are best suited to be used as shower wall coverings or backsplashes although they can also suit low foot traffic areas. They are available in a wide range of colours and finishes.

Granite, natural stone, travertine, marble and slate can produce wonderful finishes. They are available in a wide range of stones with various porosities, in many tile sizes and work well with super-thin joints. Terrazzo is a composite material of chips of marble, glass, granite and other materials, giving dramatic finishes. It is either pre-cast offsite and fitted or poured in-situ. Reconstituted stone is a further option. It is made from Quartz, which is mixed with polymer resins and pigments. A wide range of colors and finishes are available.

These stones can give glorious finishes and are a suitable floor covering… but in truth, are not normally selected by the cost-conscious builder.

Cement Tiles have been around from the Victorian era and are manufactured in a wide array of patterns and colours. They are porous and can be refreshed with sanding and sealing reminiscent of solid wooden floors. In high traffic areas they need regular attention and so can be a high maintenance item.

Carpets.

Carpets come in a variety of textures and finishes, and of course almost any color. As far as the fit-out is concerned, the most important issue is the thickness of the carpet when combined with the underlay. These two layers will sit on the structural floor level (SFL) and are often fitted against a baseboard also placed on the SFL. They ride up against the face of the base board and do not slip underneath like every other finish. Gripper bars are fitted to hold the carpet down against the skirting.

Laundries.

Very common in Canada & the US, I think laundries/boot-rooms are a welcome addition to any house. The larger house benefits from a coat-hanging and shoe storage area near the entrance hallway, while a washing room that is accessible from an outside area works well for families.

Design the layout much as you would the kitchen, working through each part: wall cupboards and storage places to store the ironing board, etc. Kitchen type cabinets and worktops with a large steel sink can be very useful.

Conservatories and Swimming Pools.

If desired, conservatories and swimming pools are best designed as part of the build, even if, for reason of cash-flow, they cannot be constructed at the same time as the main house. The purpose of this is so it is easier to construct the structure later. With, for example, careful placing of drains, or a planned allowance within the electrical service or even a foundation temporarily covered by garden these can all save challenging operations later when the time is right.

Solar heating can benefit pools by reducing running costs. Modern pump systems are available which generate less noise than the systems previously installed in even quite recent times. A low-level humming noise can be exasperating both to you and your neighbors.

Security.

Many designers build in security. This works best when the extra security does not inconvenience the occupants. For example, sensor lights at the main door gives you a visual look at anyone seeking entry by ringing the doorbell. The next step up is a camera entry system, so you can see and speak to the visitor before opening your door. Camera systems can also record the external areas, which can be replayed later if needed. Strong locks deter easy forced entry, with vision from a public area reducing the intruder's opportunities to hide.

Simple deterrents also work well. Try not to provide an external ladder, *by the roofs and its very structure*, allowing access to the upper floors. A lockable gate between the front and rear areas is always a deterrent. The garden can have small, thorny type bushes placed beneath windows and see-through, shoulder high fencing on the boundaries. These are all points to be worked through as part of the design, from the beginning.

Chapter 11 - Action

- Visit Kitchen and Bathroom showrooms
- Check screw centers in drywall sheets
- Check and measure everything to ensure base boards and trim can be properly fitted
- Discuss hardware in detail with your designers and contractors
- Get the kitchen and bathroom working – dimensionally
- Wardrobes and cupboards are for storing stuff – do you have enough space?

MONEY/TIME
Budget & Cash Flow
Final Account Preparation

WORKS
Finishing Is All That Is Seen
Punch Lists
Defect Correction & Sign Off

DESIGN
Fit Out Selections

CHAPTER 12
SUMMARY

What to look for and how to prevent issues when dealing with contractors.

Highlights covered in this chapter include:

- What are 'Red Flags'?
- The 'Usual Suspects'
- Information to include in tenders
- Is the offer too good to be true?
- Before you undertake any legal action!

CHAPTER 12

MAKING A 'GOOD DEAL'

'This home had more red flags than a Chinese military parade'.
— Ryan J. Gutierrez

The construction industry has more than its fair share of busy lawyers. Site disputes can be exhausting for everyone involved in the process. This usually ends up with inferior work offered, acceptable standards dropped, cost overruns incurred and delays eventuating. This is a poor outcome for a relationship which started so well.

The very nature of the industry 'breeds' disputes; a site environment where many thousands of components are worked on or fitted by various people. People who are either self-employed or work for many different companies. This all takes place at a single temporary works or 'factory' all at the same time. The opportunity for misunderstandings and fall-outs is immense, and the relatively few legal disputes occurring is a testament to the professionalism of most workers.

Your site will be occupied at various times of the day or week, with deliveries arriving for immediate use or stored for later installation. To make this happen in a positive environment takes planning and management.

Before workers or visitors attend site, they need to be inducted and instructed. Large sites often take this seriously and may require all persons entering a site to view a visual multimedia presentation on the specific site and OH&S. This can be considered a little excessive on a single house, but the principle remains. Contractors and operatives must know the ground rules. Are you enforcing a high viz policy? Where are the water and electrical supplies? Where can they park vehicles? This may seem minor but can be a major issue to your neighbors.

Keep on top of your contractors' questions and answer points on things like: what site assistance do they need? what are their scaffolding and access requirements? All workers must be clear on what they are to do, as well as when and how.

Early Warnings.

Take early indications that all is not well with a contractor seriously. The signs could be lots of little negative things all happening at once or perhaps are due to matters occurring elsewhere. The contractors will not only work on your home, they will be juggling works on other (and possibly many other) homes, depending on their trade and how busy they are. They will also be going back to previous sites to fix issues or amend something that was not quite right.

These outside events can affect your site operations. Problem's others give them that affect their cash flow, for example, can also affect you!

Look at the project overall and assess if recent site changes have had a financial effect on the contractors. I am not saying you encourage them to make a claim or increase their quote, but rather be aware. Consider all design developments as they occur, even if they are not chargeable as extras.

It is your job as owner-builder, to ensure that all needed materials are on site and available to use. In fairness to the contractors is this the case? Are new ideas regular occurrences and instructions passed over late? Or is it that, on fleshing out the works, small tweaks are arising to improve the overall quality of the completed job? All these things can be a disruptive influence on progress and morale on-site.

Red Flags.

Is the manager of a contractor or his workforce not regularly attending site?

Are valuations or applications for payments submitted in advance of the works being complete?

Are contractors seeking to make hefty charges for minor change orders… or raising lots of small or inconsequential change orders… or simply just general delays?

Points to be considered:

- Does progress as reported by the contractor through payment applications match the progress you can assess?
- Is the contractor factoring in all the outstanding works he has to complete before his works are finished?
- Can you discern if the contractor has failed to lock in prices from his suppliers?
- Do his suppliers seem to be reluctant to supply him with materials?
- Is he seeking payment for offsite materials or products?
- Is this particular contractor slipping behind the overall works schedule?
- In plain terms, is he seeking too much money for the works he has installed?
- Even with the best will in the world, has he found he cannot deliver the work for the agreed cost?
- Has he under-resourced the works and is falling behind?
- Are other contractors or workers disrupting his work flow?
- Are other projects putting strain on his finances or labor?
- Is there any confusion or issue with the Provisional Sums and their adjusted measurement?
- Is the contractor just poor at the administrative/organizational side of his business and the proper messages are not sent or received?
- Has he raised concerns over things you are not doing, like making areas ready for him to carry out his works?

Many disputes can be sourced back to the pre-site agreements and a lack of clarity. This can still occur whether there are many contractors or only a single tenderer. It is important that the risks of placing an order with each contractor is considered individually, before instruction is given and legal obligations undertaken. You always need clarity on what is expected by all parties over specifications, cost, time schedules and scope of the works. Responsibilities must be apportioned.

It can be that more than one of the aforementioned issues arises with a single contractor. This can spread to disquiet and problems with other contractors. A delay by one contractor can cascade down the schedule of works to others. Issues may occur simultaneously with more than one contractor, which can signal serious consequences for the schedules and budgets.

What Can You Do?

First of all, do not delay taking action. Tackle issues verbally with the contractor; try to see what the problem is and how best this can be resolved. Try to resolve any disputes at the most basic level you can. Consider confirming your fears in writing and seek to positively move matters on. To be clear, just because you don't confirm a point immediately in writing, it doesn't mean you should not record it at all. If matters escalate at some future time, having an accurate record of site labor, events and progress can be very important.

> **TRUE STORY**
>
> We needed to order some specialized air conditioning equipment and controls for a large project. The contractor was to supply and deliver the goods. As they were made specially for this project, the manufacturer required a large deposit in order to commence production and full payment before delivery. We were reluctant to pay over a large sum to a 'middle man' but needed the goods to carry out the works. To come up with solutions, not problems, we agreed to take over the order directly with the manufacturer. The contractor's price included a mark-up, which we paid to him. This was to cover him for costs around sourcing and placing the order. As we paid the manufacturer directly this reduced the contractor's cash-flow issues and we were at less risk. If matters had taken a bad turn and he had ceased trading before the goods were delivered, we would have been out of pocket. To cover us, if the manufacturer ceased trading, it was agreed that 'our' goods would be stored and labelled as in our ownership.

Does the contractor feel you are abusing his good nature by continuously changing your instructions? If so, decide a fixed way forward and stick to it. The contractor at management level or the operative may feel they need to protect themselves from losses. They will likely have experienced sites where multiple decisions regularly changed the scope of the works. They may even write to you and expect each change order specifically agreed and costed before they will accept an instruction. At least you know where you are and so will they.

Change Orders.

'Each and every change order should be flagged up as needing an extension of time' is a theory floated by some contractors. This is particularly the case where a completion penalty is at stake. They do this regardless of the actual delay; it is seen as a 'scene setter'. An example would be, you confirm 20 change orders and they request 20 extensions of time. You refuse all extension of time claims. Can they say on the 21st change order, the cumulative effect of the variations is such that an extension of time is well deserved overall… even though no single instruction merits this?

When you are considering claims for extensions of time and for extra money, it is wise to focus on the big items first and not get drawn into the smaller stuff initially. The smaller items can be used by you later on as bargaining points. The owner-builder should '*follow the money*', i.e. pay special attention to operations significant to on-site progress or those with the largest sums of money at stake. Calculating an updated contract sum or projected final account can help focus all parties on where they are financially and what funds remain in play to complete the works.

It could be any or all of the above or perhaps another reason for the problems but you as owner-builder will have to deal with the issue. The aim is to prevent escalation of the problem and the situation developing from a claim into a formal dispute.

You must decide what action to take. There are dangers and risks by acting, as well as by not acting. If you decide to take contractual/legal action, first reassure yourself you are within the terms of your agreement.

Both Ways Cost You.

You must contrast the cost of replacing a contractor, including the disruption this will cause, with the cost of limping on with a contractor delaying progress and perhaps not offering a reasonable standard of work. Invariably, it costs more to engage a new contractor to complete works after a failing contractor, than it does to let the original contractor complete.

It is vital you first take legal advice if you do decide to terminate a contract. It is prudent to take legal advice, even if you are only considering such a course for any reason.

Prepare a cost benefit analysis to show you the upside and downside risk of legally taking this action. And then think about it carefully some more. Usually, what to do is a finely balanced decision, however, not considering the problem and not seeking a solution invariably leads to a worse outcome.

The Usual Suspects (US)

Let's recognize and consider the 'Usual Suspects' of reasons for dispute. This may help you avoid some pitfalls and reduce the consequence of others.

All construction projects are liable to disputes or at least a feeling at some point that you have agreed something you didn't like to keep things progressing on site. You probably decided to agree after looking at the bigger picture; you tell yourself, *it's for the greater good*. You are often correct to be pragmatic and keep the momentum of site progress going. Interestingly, trade contractors, on the other side of the discussion, often feel the same. Understanding other people's issues and being empathetic does not need to mean you are walked over contractually. You are looking to diffuse points of dispute.

What are the risks, and what impact will these risks have on the whole project?

Negotiation and compromise are part of the project manager's daily work. The attitude of the manager is crucial to matters getting resolved before they escalate.

We shall consider the 'Usual Suspects' in the order of them appearing in the normal life cycle of a project. Then we will diagnose the common ailments.

Seeking Tenders.

Send out the following information to selected contractors as part of your covering letter:

- Name of Client
- Name of Architect or site project manager (if they are supervising)
- Name of relevant consultants to their works
- Name and type of project
- Location and full address of site
- Brief description
- Date for dispatch and return of tenders (timelines work!)
- Start date on site and duration (Approximate information will assist)
- Form of contract – if one exists or is to be signed or followed

- General conditions applying to the contract
- Particular conditions applying to contract
- Specification of works or drawing comprehensively detailing works

US 1 – Specification.

It is crucial all contractors, for a single works package, to be issued with identical information for tender purposes. Regardless of how many works packages you seek prices for, each and every package must be complete and state what works are required and which are to be priced.

Relate the quality and standard of works to a national standard or code of practice. These standards are industry wide and act as a benchmark for the acceptable quality of works or materials offered. If certification from an outside body or self-certification is required, this can be set out and sought as part of the works.

In fact, the job will not be considered complete without the issue of the certificates. Certificates are not to be held back as a hostage for payment; they are an intrinsic part of the agreed delivery.

As a general rule, the greater the detail, the higher the cost of providing the information. Spreadsheets and schedules can provide information to supplement drawings and specification notes.

US 2 - Access to the Works.

This is a two-way street – what access will you offer and what access equipment will the supplier/contractor offer or require? At its simplest, state *how* access will be offered to your site and from which roads, etc. Include any conditions of working times the local authority has imposed through planning conditions. For example, it is common that time restrictions for works cannot commence before 8.00am and must not extend after 6.00pm Monday to Friday with restricted working times over the weekend.

During summer seasons, the work crew may prefer to start earlier to take advantage of the cooler temperature earlier in the day. Perhaps the opposite is the case during the winter months. Can they be accommodated without disturbing the neighbors?

You can ask if the contractor has special access requirements. This can include for cranes, hoists, concrete pumps, dumper trucks, excavators, etc. If a cost is to be incurred, it needs to be clear if the contractor has included for it… or are you expected to provide the access or equipment?

> **TIP BOX**
>
> It will pay dividends for you to meet the neighbors around your boundary and slightly beyond and provide them with contact details for the on-site representative. This is best dealt with by actual owner-builder talking to actual residents, not communications coming from a remote office.

US 3 - Equipment to be Provided.

This can be a matter for agreement or normal procedure for the contractor.

It is usual and expected for the owner-builder to provide some common site equipment to all contractors. This includes OH&S features, such as safety handrails around openings, site power to different areas of the site, and site lighting. Toilet facilities and site-dependent welfare facilities, such as sheds or canteen areas, are to be provided.

General rubbish dumpsters are provided for all contractors to dispose of waste. It is normal for contractors to dispose of waste if a dumpster is conveniently located and to tidy up around their work area. Often, they will expect owner-builder supplied labor to keep the site clean and remove waste from their own site area to the disposal point. If you want it otherwise, you must state this requirement. It will not be implied.

It is necessary for all contractors to work to the same information regarding levels and grids. It is the owner-builder's responsibility to provide this information to the contractors. If you are not skilled at transferring levels and setting grids, employ a professional surveyor or setting out engineer. To be clear, provide levels unless you are satisfied the contractor can competently transfer them.

More detail can be added to the contract as to how the contractor will specifically provide his equipment. For example, will access scaffolding be provided by you or will the contractor work off their own tower scaffolds?

Equipment and material agreements can be arranged on an individual basis with each contractor. For example, a bricklayer will not provide the bricks or the sand and cement for the mortar, unless by specific agreement. Sometimes the owner-builder supplies the mixing equipment, other times the bricklayer does.

These agreements have flow-on effects. Look at the risk/reward situation if the bricklayer provides the mixing equipment and mortar mix. If the equipment is not sufficiently efficient or breaks down, who is responsible for incurred costs? Equally, if the sand is delivered late and bricks cannot be laid, who incurs the cost? However, a 'smaller' contractor may provide a more competitive price if the owner-builder provides the site equipment. The bricks, as a large cost item, are invariably supplied by the owner-builder.

The principles above apply to all other contractors too, e.g. the concreting contractor. The owner-builder usually supplies the ready-mix concrete and concrete pump to the concreters but not their ply for shuttering. The whole issue is site specific and based on what is accepted local practice in your region. The key is to be clear on your's and your contractors' part of the agreement.

To tackle this, be definite on what you are providing, or alternatively, provide the design information and carefully read the tenders to see what is offered. Whichever way, you must be clear on who provides what before placing an order.

US 4 – Information and Variations.

Information on building projects changes rapidly. It's quite common for information and instructions to be revised. In this case, change orders must be issued immediately to contractors. Drawings and schedules are numbered individually and each revision is noted as such and dated. This provides a timeline of when variation drawings were issued. Not all change orders are cost increasing or decreasing. Some change orders are cost neutral, although each should be considered.

Try not to just issue documents and assume all has been received and fully understood. Engage with the contractor and go over the instruction to ensure the changes are understood and all implications are included going forward.

Consider if the variation will:

- Increase cost
- Delay a stage or completion of the works

- Be outside of the original scope
- When taken in context with other change orders amount to 'scope creep.'

And are you prepared to confirm the change order in writing if requested to do so by the contractor?

The contractor is well within his rights to seek confirmation of variations and seek agreement to specific increased sums before he proceeds with the work.

What about the final sums? It is good practice to re-evaluate each contractor's projected final account before each payment is made. By monitoring ongoing and projected costs you are in control of your finances.

Cost projections for the whole project do not need to be shared with the contractor but sharing agreed variations for their element of the works allows them to maintain their cost control procedures. You will get a sense of how far you should go along this road and what level of information sharing is appropriate for each contractor. Update the contractors in broad terms on the overall construction schedule and what is time critical as far as their works are concerned.

US 5 - Design Information.

If the contractor is to supply calculations or other design information as part of the agreement of works, this must be received in sufficient time for checking.

Q: Why check a contractor's calculations when you do not check your consultant's calculations?

A: The consultant is appointed by you to act for you – whereas a contractor provides you with a competitive figure to win your work. You must to establish that their design meets the regulations and meets your functioning needs. Will his plan and solution work for you?

For the owner-builder, it can be attractive for elements to be manufactured off-site and delivered complete for installation. The manufacturers of off-site components and pods are usually very good at providing information on their products and give advice on fixing on site.

US 6 – Standards.

National and international standards are created to ensure compliance with a whole raft of legislation. These are often supplemented by codes of practice and possibly rigorous testing off and on-site.

Off-site testing relates to standards to be achieved by the product and are confirmed by the engraving, printing or labelling of a quality certification mark to show users the materials comply.

On-site testing confirms an installation meets a pre-set standard; records of tests are produced and a certificate issued confirming compliance.

It's important to familiarize yourself with the elements of installations requiring certification. Confirm what information must be checked and recorded. The inclusion of non-approved materials or unavailability of certificates can delay the completion and occupation of your home. Non-compliant items, for whatever reason, may need to be changed, and the later in the process this occurs, the more it costs.

US 7 - Interdependent Services.

Take care when compiling and detailing the services packages in particular. Services, namely, water, solar, air conditioning, gas, heating, telephone, TV, intercom, security, Wi-Fi, fire protection, passenger elevator, indoor cinemas, etc. are all interdependent. They all require power from the electrical service and cannot work without it. This leads to cross-over zones between contractors at each and every connection point. So, it must be absolutely clear who does what.

US 8 - Schedule of Works.

A contract schedule should be maintained and regularly updated by the owner-builder. By updating the schedule, issues of concern will be highlighted before they escalate. This 'window on the future' can be invaluable in recognizing issues with potential disputes and dealing with them before they are allowed to happen. By linking the Contract Schedule to your projected cashflows, it metaphorically shouts out to you if something is wrong.

US 9 - Too Good to be True...

Sometimes a price received is lower than you can reasonably expect when compared to other contractors' prices. Rather than gleefully accepting the quotation, investigate why this is.

There can be many reasons for the variance. Has the contractor a method of delivery uniquely making them cheaper than everyone else, or a special deal with a supplier, giving him a competitive advantage?

Just as likely, he has not included all you require in his works package... or is working to lesser standards. If all items are not included, will they be looking for change orders to increase their contract sum as soon as the order has been placed? Are they experienced in your kind of project and have they made sufficient allowances? A contractor may provide a more competitive price based on a very quick on-site time. They may say they scheduled and priced to be on-site for say, one week. If not all items of others' work are complete and they are delayed to say, two weeks on site, will they be looking for compensation for the extra costs?

Usually if something is too good to be true, it is. Be as careful of underbidding as you would overbidding.

US 10 - Contract Arrangements.

Legal contracts are entered into by all of us every day. For example, a small transaction, like buying a book from a retailer is a contract. The book is advertised at a price (the offer) you pick it up and take it to the counter and complete the purchase (acceptance). By paying, you recognize a consideration. Even if the agreement is only a verbal agreement, previous case law will cover the situation. As constructing a house is such a large project, you are legally better covered if you have a written agreement in place.

Your intention is to be clear on what you are instructing the other party to do and this is best achieved by avoiding vague terms. You wish to create a binding agreement that an outside party can fully understand. Clarity is all.

To be valid, all contracts must contain each of the following three items:

Offer.

By seeking a tender from a contractor, you are inviting an offer. When the contractor provides a tender, you can choose to accept the offer or not. If you do accept, then the matter of the value is agreed. If you do not accept, the matter may be negotiated and if agreement is reached, the previous offer is superseded and the agreed sum becomes the offer.

Acceptance.

Once an offer agreeable to both parties has been made, the parties following best practice, formally exchange acceptance by a written order. If this is done, it clarifies the situation in a way a verbal acceptance cannot. If one party accepts the order without written confirmation but commences works on site, it can be deemed that the offer was accepted and the contracted agreement is in place. In this situation, no written form of agreement was made, so only the most basic legal safeguards can be relied upon.

Consideration.

All contracts must have a consideration, usually financial, but it's not necessary for it to be a consideration at a recognised commercial 'going rate'. The easiest way forward is to agree a sum or rate for the works and this is included as part of the agreement.

US 11 - Contract Documents.

Arrangements are dealt with by a standard set of formal contract documents, which are widely adopted by the construction industry in your region. A standard document can be signed and the agreements followed as laid down. These standard contracts can be amended to meet the precise conditions of individual projects. Seek specialist advice from your consultants or legal advisor before agreements are made or amended.

Consider the type of input a contractor is providing and if a formal contractual agreement is needed. This decision will be based on the suitability in each case and also on the amount of risk you feel comfortable with. Against all lawyer's advice it is not appropriate in a single house project for all contractors to be offered written formal contracts. Some contractors would consider such a document strange and unusual. They would expect you to stick to your word and they will stick to theirs. You must assess who you are dealing with and act accordingly.

US 12 - Chasing Redress.

Pursuing legal redress is not appropriate under certain financial levels as it can be more expensive to legally proceed than not. In the end, you must consider if you will get legal satisfaction, let alone financial compensation. In law, the ends often do not justify the cost of the means. If it's a close financial call, chalk it up to experience and although you may be disappointed, move on with your life and project.

Contractors and suppliers often have their own legal conditions they want you to agree to before they will accept your instruction. Read these carefully and only agree with the conditions when you are satisfied all is in order. If you are unhappy with any clauses, seek advice and perhaps offer to vary the contract agreement before you legally commit.

Standard contracts and contractors' conditions usually cover the following points:

- Payment Terms
- Delays
- Dispute Resolution Methods
- Inclement Weather
- Authorized Signatories

Payment Terms must be agreed as part of the instruction. If, after agreement, any changes in circumstances occur, the owner-builder must inform the contractor and seek agreement as to how matters will proceed.

If a contractor's work is delayed through no fault of theirs and costs are incurred, the contractor may seek recompense. Equally, the contractor may be liable if he causes delay and the owner-builder may seek recompense.

Alternative Dispute Resolution methods are set out as the preferred method of resolution over legal procedures. At least be familiar with the process; if not, you are agreeing to something you do not understand.

Inclement Weather is a point of common debate when discussing outside activities and is often cited as a reason for delay. It is predictable and normal that the weather will vary and this must be accepted by all parties. Weather can only be accepted as a reason for delay if it is unseasonably or exceptionally inclement. The fact it rained on a specific day is not unexpected, as annually it rains on many days. It must be shown the weather had unexpectedly affected site progress.

Climate scientists are currently saying that previously predicted 100-year weather events can now be expected every 50-years. This means the calculated likelihood of work-stopping weather conditions has doubled since the existing forms of contract were originally written.

Authorized Signatories should only ever sign a contract. Ensure you know who you are dealing with. Do background checks on the directors of companies and look for comments on the company's performance on social media. Will the directors be signing the contract or is it a partnership and all partners are required to sign the contract? You do not want to be in the position of entering into a contract with someone signing who is not authorized. Or not everyone who was needed to has signed in order to make the document legally enforceable. Your lawyer should advise on this.

Both the best form of defense and attack is based on records. Records of instructions, variations, schedule updates and payments must be meticulously kept. A site diary and a note of conversations can be very useful when you are looking back from a future point. Regular time-dated images can show more than reams of written information. The more specific the information, the more useful it will be.

Only sign the contract if you believe it is entirely correct.

US 13 - Letters of 'Intent'.

These are a halfway house type arrangement, where the client wants to get works started or materials on order but all the contractual arrangements are not yet agreed or are not yet in place. In this circumstance, the owner-builder can formally write to the contractor/supplier to ask for works to commence within a detailed and limited scope. The writer commits to cover costs incurred, or better still, an agreed sum, if the order is rescinded. Always include a start and end date as time restrictions are useful. Do not issue one of these without your lawyer's advice. Be aware that this letter is a 'legal' document and full consideration must be given to all aspects.

US 14 - Is it All There?

This is the most basic check you can perform, and yet often the most telling. The owner-builder must check in detail what was not included and think through the implications of what was not included. You may consider the process of pondering *what is not there* peculiar, but what is not there can add significantly to costs and delays.

The only way to know if something is not included is by understanding the process of what must be done, and therefore, what was specifically stated as included. If items are not mentioned by name, query and confirm their inclusion.

An example of this is a description to build a brick wall. Is the wall to be built and finished with a pointed joint, or raked out and left? It is far better to be thorough and seek confirmation over this item, even if the contractor may consider the pointing is implied.

You can never be sure what anyone else is thinking, but by checking the details, you can avoid a dispute later.

Sometimes, an offer is for a portion or package of works covering a range of items. Do try to be as specific as you reasonably can and also seek confirmation of their acceptance that it is a fixed price and lump sum for an amount of work. This could be, for example, externally painting the whole house. This is an attempt to include all items needed, not only those specifically mentioned. In this case, a non-mentioned item is deemed included. The agreed contract is for the whole job and an agreed amount, which will not change unless the scope of works changes.

The owner-builder must be watchful and if needed, ask themselves *why* there is a proliferation of change orders. These must be assessed to determine if the changes are actual changes that have a financial effect or non-chargeable design developments.

Often contractors are poor at providing timely information and place more importance on the works than the administration side of their business. What you must *not* do is try to buy your way out of trouble, as it is invariably money down the tubes.

What can you do if you consider there has been a breach of contract?

Before you resort to legal action, work out exactly:

- What was the breach?
- What specifically went wrong?
- Who committed the breach?
- It is crucial you are clear on exactly who the offending party is; who signed the contract?
- Was it signed by Directors of the company?
- Was it signed by a partnership and did both partners sign?
- Are all signatures witnessed?

What loss have you suffered?

- Can you show actual loss?
- This loss must be calculated and not generic

Is the offending party solvent?

- There is no point seeking damages from someone who is bankrupt. You will never get repaid.

Should you seek urgent legal advice?

- Yes.

US 15 – Performance.

In the end, the 'Good Deal' is achieved when both parties to the contract are satisfied or can accept the outcome. Both parties need to perform as they promised or otherwise the contract is in difficulty and the offended party need not comply. Do you both have different opinions on the values of changed items? If so, look to agree on these or seek a third party to mediate.

If the contractor does not install an effective system that meets the agreement or specification, or worse, does not work at all, then the 'employer' only has to pay for the benefit he received from the works. If the 'employer' does not, for example, make payments as agreed, the contractor does not have to perform until payments are made.

The whole chapter above is taking you places you do not want to be. Be aware of what a 'Good Deal' is to you.

If you are ever tempted to break a contract and seek legal redress, regardless of which side you are on – do not do it – not until you have taken clear and cool-headed legal advice. I've found that the whole process can be torturous. I have over the years, reluctantly, been involved in a few disputes and each one is one too many. They are distracting and time consuming and as far as I am concerned, the pain has always outweighed the benefits. However, with nowhere else to turn, you must be prepared to keep the lawyers busy!

The wisest advice if a problem arises is to open the dialogue at the lowest level possible and deal with the issue then and there. Take a reality check; this is a single project and your future home. How can you get from where you are, to completion?

> **TIP BOX**
>
> Good advice if you want to fail spectacularly:
>
> Do Not seek competitive prices
> Do Not set out the scope of the works
> Do Not agree a fixed sum or rates for the works
> Do Not consider schedule matters or an end date for the works
> Do Not agree the specification for the works
> Do Not benchmark the specification to National Standards
> Do Not prepare the area for the contractor
> Do Not give timely instructions
> Do Not confirm change orders
> Do Not use the terminology used in the agreement
> Do Not make regular payments in line with the agreement
> Do Not accept increases in cost regardless of merit
> Do Not correspond with the contractor
> Do Not follow the process laid out in the unsigned Contract
> *Do resort to legal action as the first option*

Chapter 12 – Action

- Take advice on the appropriateness of contracts
- Talk to your on-site contractors every day
- Resolve all queries/disputes at site level before escalating up the chain
- Keep records of instructions, variations, schedule updates, and payments
- Keep on top of costs, you will know what a good deal is

CHAPTER 13
SUMMARY

By knowing what Alternative Dispute Resolution (ADR) is, you can judge if it is of benefit in your circumstances.

Highlights covered in this chapter include:

- What is ADR?
- Independent Person
- Mediation
- Conciliation
- Adjudication
- Arbitration

CHAPTER 13

ALTERNATIVE DISPUTE RESOLUTION (ADR)

'Everybody has a plan until they get punched in the mouth'.
– Mike Tyson

In Chapter 12, Making A 'Good Deal', many of the pitfalls of relationship management are set out, with strategies and tactics to keep matters moving along with various contractors and suppliers. It is best if your project avoids any involvement with the legal process, but it is important for all owner-builders to have a basic understanding of what it is and what it involves.

ADR refers to legal procedures that are a speedier and cheaper form of justice over and above full litigation through the courts. Alternatives to a legal system that is bewildering to most of us and expensive for all parties is always a good thing. When you sign a contract, you are often agreeing to embrace ADR as a means of resolving disputes if they arise and cannot be dealt with directly by the parties. This chapter provides a flavour of what ADR has become.

The top cause of construction disputes globally are all parties, Owner/ Contractor/ Specialist Contractors, not understanding their contractual obligations. This means that they do not treat others as they are meant to. By thinking about what you have to do and communicating calmly with all the other parties in a two-way conversation, this can be mainly eliminated. This simple act can transform the site and radically improve performance and quality.

You may, however, feel a separation of interests between you and the other party. The quality of the works or 'the good of the job' are not at the forefront of what others are trying to do. You have fundamental differences of opinion and you feel annoyed. These feelings move you to consider that a formal dispute process is an option. 'Feelings' can drive you to taking decisions that a calmer review may rule out. However, we are people and not machines, and feelings can sometimes sway you into actions that in retrospect may not have been the wisest move overall. Think carefully and do not act in haste. All forms of legal action are stressful… and rarely satisfying.

In some states and provinces, the route for disputes are laid out and need to be followed. These states and provinces list specific options on how to proceed with the dispute and the way forward to seeking resolution. Quebec, Alberta and Ontario have legislation that requires ADR before litigation is commenced but the other Provinces do not a *require* 'settlement conferences,' it's just good advice. In all states and provinces, you must follow your lawyer's advice, the signed contract and common sense.

Alternative Dispute Resolution (ADR) describes procedures that are an alternative to litigation through the courts and is always the preferred legal route. Building contracts usually reference ADR as a remedy and yet most of us don't know what it is. Remember, it puts you at a disadvantage if you sign something you do not understand.

You may feel that matters are at a point where a form of ADR is required. Sometimes you feel you have to fight them on the *breaches*.

All types of 'Party-to-Party' negotiation can save time and are cost efficient when compared to the much longer and more expensive process of litigation. Courts can order ADR where they perceive it can be of assistance and thus free up their schedules. Indeed, judges in legal proceedings regularly question why ADR was not undertaken before the case was referred to them. Any party refusing to go through ADR may find their case disadvantaged.

Therefore, opportunities to come to an agreement outside of the formal court process should be thoroughly investigated.

Parties seeking resolution can seek ADR at any stage and it does not have to be written into a contract before it is appropriate. Willingness to compromise early in a dispute is the number one cure to stopping things before they start.

Do not take this chapter as an alternative to current legal advice. Take due notice of your legal advisors and only use this information to set the scene.

Who Do You Call?

ADR professionals who are trained in construction disputes often have a background in a legal or construction profession. Many are experienced and qualified in both worlds. The method of appointment of an ADR professional may well be named in the contract agreement or both parties can agree on a suitable person. The Chartered Institute of Arbitrators can advise on suitable members as can professional associations such as Royal Architects Institute of Canada (RAIC), American Institute of Architects (AIA) or Royal Institute of Chartered Surveyors (RICS).

Most insurance companies covering design professionals and builders require that you undergo a type of ADR as part of the settlement procedure. You should inform them of the dispute and they may well be able to assist by either taking over the legal dispute or by providing guidance over your approach to ADR professionals.

Independent Person.

After things go wrong, it can become difficult to reach an understanding or agreement with the other party. As an alternative to both you and your opposite number going to war, a way forward can be to bring in an independent person that both parties can trust to act fairly. This can take the 'heat' out of discussions. An independent professional known to both sides can be agreed as suitable to mediate. This could be a consultant on the project who is prepared to help out or another independent and knowledgeable person. Alternatively, it can be a person unknown to both sides who comes to the dispute with an open mind.

Mediation.

Mediation is a formal process where an independent person tries to mediate between two parties. The mediator will try to get both parties to understand the other's position and see if the situation can be resolved by concession or accommodation on both sides. This will not work unless both parties accept that a perfect agreement can be elusive and an acceptable compromise may be needed to conclude the matter. The mediator has no power to impose a solution and therefore encourages both parties to compromise.

Try to appoint a mediator experienced in the area of the dispute, someone familiar with the industry and accepted norms. The mediator brings a combination of common sense, patience and persistence, and looks to work alongside both parties to resolve the dispute.

The mediator will often look to the future, predicting outcomes the participants can expect if the case is not resolved. They are not so concerned with strict legal rights. In effect they will, often through separate private discussion, try to deliver a reality check to both parties.

The mediator cannot offer legal advice but can assist in framing and wording an agreement and expand the settlement options for both parties.

The mediation agreement will be the only record of the mediation and so parties receive confidentiality throughout. The mediator cannot be brought before later proceedings to comment on the process.

This means there is an element of safety for all concerned, as the process remains confidential and cannot be referenced in open correspondence. If the mediation is successful, all well and good. If matters do not succeed, then mediation will not affect later proceedings.

Mediations can be arranged within a few days and can be located through national mediation services.

Overall, mediation is the most cost effective and confidential form of ADR and can allow resolution much earlier than litigation. Both parties agree to pay their own costs. As the mediation is scheduled and completed over a limited timeframe, costs are manageable and predictable.

Conciliation.

Conciliation is similar to mediation and effectively takes place in an almost identical manner. Conciliators, however, can offer advice and guidance and make suggestions as to how matters can be agreed. Both parties may well have to moderate their position but they will consider a tabled way forward, with potential options for agreement.

Adjudication.

Adjudication is taking the matter in dispute out of both party's hands and seeking resolution from an experienced, independent and impartial person.

The person who starts the process by submitting a 'Notice of Adjudication' can put forward the expertise they are looking for in an adjudicator. The background often requested is legal, architectural or surveying. The initial notice is followed up by a 'Referral Notice'. The aim of this is to set out clearly the matters in dispute, attaching relevant documentation. The responding party comes back with their defence and any further documentation. Once all the relevant documents and points are made, the Adjudicator will consider and issue their decision. The whole process can usually be completed in four to six weeks.

The adjudicator's decision is binding and limits the parties from proceeding onto further litigation. At adjudication, both parties agree to pay their own costs regardless of the outcome.

Adjudication is a speedy process when compared with other forms of legal remedy and this speed can be a limiting factor to how much depth the case goes into. Nearly always, the only evidence is in written form. The adjudicator may undertake a site visit if deemed necessary, but there will not be an opportunity for either side to verbally put their case or have witnesses questioned. Though a faster form of resolution than the courts, parties can feel matters are not exhaustively examined and nuances are overlooked. Put bluntly, it can seem a rough form of justice. As the adjudication process is intense, sufficient time and resource needs to be available.

Arbitration.

Arbitration is the most formal of the recommended ADR routes. This process calls for detailed arguments and so will hold a tribunal to review both sides' positions. They then rule on the basis of material facts, documents, witnesses and principles of law. The arbitration process is binding on all parties and is a quicker and cheaper method of reaching a conclusion than litigation.

The process is usually initiated by one party sending the other a written demand for arbitration. This highlights what the dispute is over and what remedy is sought. The receiving party can respond, indicating in writing if they accept the matter is suitable for arbitration. Many formal contracts indicate arbitration is the most suitable process of ADR.

Much of the process of arbitration is similar to, but a lesser form of, full scale litigation. In arbitration, fees can be awarded by the arbitrator.

All forms of ADR can be complex and stressful to all participants, though the whole process is designed to be cheaper and less gruelling than full litigation. Seek legal advice before any form of ADR is undertaken, particularly if adjudication or arbitration is considered. Through discussion, all involved can seek to resolve the problem or make a judgement call.

It is hoped all parties realise a simple truth: the longer a dispute goes on, the more it costs.

Increased information sharing by Building Information Management (BIM) and other associated knock-on improvements has statistically reduced the number of disputes year-on-year. The reasons for this are still a point of discussion although it seems that BIM has formalised information sharing and effectively tracks variations and instructions. By keeping on top of these and the following financial implications has better informed all parties . The process of how you 'got here' is clearer and the clarity has reduced the number of formal disputes. You may not have all the latest technology available to your project, but you can take the lesson and communicate.

Chapter 13 – Action

This chapter is a brief overview and I strongly suggest legal advice is taken before embarking on any action at all.

- Communication throughout the process stops disputes occurring
- Be willing to compromise 'for the good of the job'
- Think about it, then before you do anything, think about it again

MONEY/TIME
Budget & Cash Flow
Final Account Preparation

WORKS
Finishing Is All That Is Seen
Defect (Snag/Punch) Lists
Defect Correction And Sign Off

DESIGN
Fit Out Selections

CONCLUSION

'It is not the critic who counts; not the man who points out how the strong man stumbles, or where the doer of deeds could have done them better. The credit belongs to the man who is actually in the arena, whose face is marred by dust and sweat and blood; who strives valiantly; who errs, who comes short again and again, because there is no effort without error and shortcoming; but who does actually strive to do the deeds; who knows great enthusiasms, the great devotions; who spends himself in a worthy cause; who at the best knows in the end the triumph of high achievement, and who at the worst, if he fails, at least fails while daring greatly, so that his place shall never be with those cold and timid souls who neither know victory nor defeat'.

– Theodore Roosevelt.

The journey is special to you.

Every house and project is different, although they all share so much in common.

None of the houses built since the time of the classic architects of the Victorian era actually design and have made special, one-off fittings. The world has adopted a system of manufacturers making pre-built fittings and materials that we can select and incorporate in our buildings.

The choice is huge, with imports from all over the world now readily available through local suppliers. The question is, what design do we want and which fittings and materials are selected to give us a unique combination; to form the home of our choice. We can choose to buy single fittings and place them together, or parts or are 'pods' built off-site and delivered complete.

This virtually unlimited choice allows us to put together the largest ever variation of new build and refurbishment styles. But a few things are forever with us. The *organized builder* will still produce the finest finish. The *big picture builder* will see the end game and get there quicker. The *uncompromising builder* will know quality matters and understand the job needs to be done right. The builder who learns from others will not make as many mistakes.

You may think *your* build is different, *your* contractors are different, and it is too hard to go the extra mile to seek only the best. However, your build is not different, and only by you taking responsibility and giving leadership can the job be done properly. Do not underestimate the power of communication. If you give an instruction, be prepared for the consequence. The opposite is also true; if you do not give an instruction, be prepared for the consequence.

Never be afraid to do the right thing. Once your contractors understand your stance, they can support you (or argue against it). Most people like being involved in high-quality workmanship as they get a kick out of doing a good job and the quality of their work acknowledged. Always strive to lead your contractors and manage your build. Be wary of cutting corners just to get finished, as it nearly always comes back to bite you.

The owner-builder has to be a quick learner. Often a mix of instinct and humility, backed up by advice from a team of professionals, means it all works out well in the end.

So, this home building journey is not for the faint hearted, but it is an experience you will always remember. And perhaps repeat.

WOMEN IN CONSTRUCTION

'A lot of people are afraid to say what they want. That's why they don't get what they want'.

– Madonna

Much has been written over many years encouraging women to enter the construction industry. Yet, in four advanced construction nations, UK, US, Canada and Australia, the number of females in construction hovers around the 10 percent mark. Obviously, this means the male construction employment rate is around 90 percent. Of the on-site operatives, the figure for females given by the US Bureau of Labor Statistics in 2018 was 3.4%. This means that males accounted for 96.6%. I believe these figures to be a fair representation for all four countries. The Canterbury region in New Zealand promotes the employment of women and claims, 16% are female within the construction industry. NZ women however, make up just 1% of registered house builders.

If you are female and an owner-builder, then may I extend you a warm welcome.

For many years, I have worked with charities and training agencies which encourage women to seek work in the construction industry. But it must be said, there is not much evidence of rising numbers of women participating as operatives, for whatever reason.

I encourage women to join the construction industry. I look forward to a time of greater equality of numbers and when women are at last rising to executive positions in many male-dominated organizations.

It is worth noting the increasing number of females joining the ranks of all the construction professions. In line with wider society, many women have led their professional bodies as President or CEO.

Long may this continue.

GENERAL GLOSSARY

Acrylonitrile-butadiene-styrene (ABS)	Material used to manufacture rigid plastic plumbing pipes.
Air Rights	The ownership of space above a building.
Anthropometrics	Measuring 'typical' humans for design purposes.
Artificial Intelligence (AI)	Artificial Intelligence (AI) is intelligence demonstrated by machines with a level of reasoning or knowledge. This often allows objects to be manipulated or moved.
Augmented Reality (AR)	Augmented Reality (AR) is often confused with VR, although the key difference is that the computer-generated information enhances perception of reality and is not completely based on virtual information.
Austenitic Stainless Steel	Type of Stainless Steel (SS) which is non magnetic and has a high resistance to corrosion.
Back Land	Land that does not have "street frontage" - accessed by a secondary road or lane.
Battleaxe	Back land which opens out in a 'battleaxe' shape.
Bridging Finance	Temporary loan to alleviate a specific financial need.
Brownfield	A site with history of previous construction.
Buildability/ Constructability	Integrate construction techniques to make the build simpler and more efficient.

Building Control Approval	Approval that all is built to national and local codes/standards.
Cesspool	A tank which collects effluent.
Competent person	A person who can identify hazards and has authorization to take action.
Compliant Permission	A planning permission designed around the regulations.
Computer Aided Design (CAD)	A digital technical drawing computer program.
Covenants	A limit or guide to future development.
Critical Path	A sequence of operations to most efficiently guide works.
Cut-in Sites	A site that lends itself to a house being built into an existing hill or slope.
Dead Load/Live Load	Dead Load - Weight of structure. Live Load - Weight of people or stored equipment or furniture.
Defects List	List of defect works aka Punch List or Snag List.
Designed for Manufacture and Assembly (DFMA)	An item designed for both ease of manufacture and assembly.
Discharging Conditions	Compliance with planning conditions.
Dormer Windows	A window that protrudes from a sloping roof.
Drywall	Sheet of gypsum plaster covered with paper, aka plasterboard, sheetrock, wallboard, gypsum (wall) board.
Earth Sheltered	A partially earth covered home.
Easements	A right to crossover or shared access to a piece of land.
Enabling Works	Works carried out to allow other works to occur.
Ergonomics	Efficiency is considered in design.

Firring Piece (Furring US)	A wedge shaped batten fixed to produce a fall to a level surface.
Flood Plain	Land prone to flooding.
Goal Gradients	A perception of advancement that encourages achievement.
Green House/Green Construction	Environmentally responsible construction.
Greenfield	A plot previously undeveloped except for agricultural use.
Hardwall	An undercoat plaster for use on masonry.
Hope Value	A value increased by expectation.
Invert Level	The level of the lowest internal surface of a drain.
Land Reclamation	Creating 'dry' land from raising the height or pumping out water from a marsh or river/sea bed.
Land Rehabilitation	Environmental remediation returning land to previous condition.
Leverage (Lever)	Using borrowed capital for investment purposes.
Lifetime Homes	Design that can be altered to accommodate physical change in occupants.
Method Statement	Written document describing the process of a specific task.
Modern Methods of Construction (MMC)	Homes constructed offsite in 3D modules.
Neutral Air Quality	A level of design and build that does not reduce current air quality.
Option Agreement	A legal document that outlines a possible enforceable option.
Outline Advice	Advice that in principle indicates what should be acceptable and achievable.
Owner - Build	Built by the property owner.

Penetrations	Holes made by services through a finished surface e.g. floor or roof.
Performance Gap	Difference between predicted and actual performance.
Plat Maps	A map showing boundary locations and important local information.
Pods	Modules produced through volumetric construction.
Punch list	Defects list.
R-Value	A measure of how well a material resists heat conduction.
Radon Gas	Radioactive gas that naturally occurs underground.
Reduction Creep	Reduction in scope of a project.
Residual Valuation	Process valuing the a development when complete.
Restricted/Unrestricted planning	Use is either restricted to a specific use or without any pre-determined restriction.
Robotics	Design and operation of robots.
Scope Creep	Incremental increase in scope of a project.
Sedum	A large variety of flowering plants- used as a roof covering.
Self-Build	Building for one's self. See Owner-Build.
Septic System	A septic tank treats the effluent and requires a suitable local outfall.
Slump Test	A measure of the consistency of fresh concrete.
Smart Home Technology (SHT)	Using automation in a residential setting.
Snag Sheet	See Defects List.
Spacers	Plastic or concrete device that sets a distance between rebar sheets or from the external surface.

Structural Members	Primary load bearing components.
Subdivision	A site divided to take more than a single home.
Sump	A low point to collect matter by gravity.
Sustainability	To avoid depletion of a resource.
Three Dimensional (3D)	Made in a solid form (Height x Width x Depth).
Tranches	Divided into parts, especially money.
U-Values	A rate of heat transfer through a material or structure from inside to outside.
Virtual Reality (VR)	A simulated feeling and look of what something would be like.
Volumetric/Modular	Constructing 3D units in factory conditions.
Water Run Off	Water flowing over the ground surface.
Virtual Reality (VR)	A simulated feeling and look of what something would be like
Volumetric/Modular	Constructing 3D units in factory conditions.
Water Run Off	Water flowing over the ground surface.

ABBREVIATIONS

3D	Three dimensional
4IR	4th Industrial Revolution
ABC	A Builders Companion
ABC (2)	Always Be Careful
ABS	Acrylonitrile-butadiene-styrene
ACM	Asbestos Containing Materials
ADA	Americans with Disability Act
ADR	Alternative Dispute Resolution
ADU's	Accessory Dwelling Units
AFSS	Automatic Fire Suppression Systems
AI	Artificial Intelligence
AI (2)	Architects Instruction
AIA	American Institute of Architects
ANSI	American National Standards Institute
APA	American Planning Association
APHA	Australian Passive House Association
AR	Augmented Reality
BAL	Bushfire Attack Level
BCA	Building Code of Australia
BER	Building Energy Rating
BIM	Building Information Modelling
BSI	British Standards Institute
CAD	Computer Aided Design

CAV	Community Asset Value
CBN	Canadian Brownfields Network
CC&Rs	Covenants, Conditions and Restrictions
CIOB	Chartered Institute of Building
CIP	Canadian Institute of Planners
CLT	Cross Laminated Timber
CMHC	Canada Mortgage and Housing Corporation
CPSF	Cost per square foot
CPVC	Chlorinated Polyvinyl Chloride
DC/AC	Direct and Alternating Current
DEAP	Dwelling Energy Assessment Procedure
DER	Dwelling Emission Rate
DFMA	Designed for Manufacture and Assembly
DTIR	Debt to Income Ratio
DWV	Drain Waste Vent
ECI	Early Contractor Involvement aka IPD
EGNH	EnerGuide for New Homes
EMF	Electromotive Force
EOI	Expression of Interest
EPC	Energy Performance Certificate
ESD	Environmentally Sustainable Design
FES	Future Energy Scenarios
FF&E	Furniture, Finishes and Equipment
FFL	Finish Floor Level
FHA	Federal Housing Administration
FRR	Fire Resistance Rating
FSC	Forest Stewardship Council
GDV	Gross Development Value
GIS	Geographic Information Systems
HEMS	Home Energy Management System
HERS	House Energy Rating Scheme

HOA	Homeowners Association
HVAC	Heating, Ventilation and Air Conditioning
IBC	International Building Code
IPD	Integrated Project Delivery aka ECI
IRC	International Residential Code
KoP	Kit of Parts
KYC	Know Your Client
LEED	Leadership on Energy and Environmental Design
LEP	Local Environment Plan
LINZ	Land Information New Zealand
Low E	Low Emissivity Glass
LVR	Loan to Value Ratio
MBIE	The Ministry of Business, Innovation and Employment
MGP	Machine Graded Pine
MIG	Metal Inert Gas
MLS	Multiple Listing Sites
MMC	Modern Methods of Construction
MOU	Memorandum of Understanding
MPAC	Municipal Property Assessment Corporation
NALFA	North American Laminate Flooring Association
NatHERS	National House Rating Scheme
NBCC	National Building Code of Canada
NHER	National Home Energy Rating
NIOSH	National Institute for Occupational Safety and Health
NOFMA	National Oak Flooring Manufacturers Association
NRZ	Neutral Reach Zones
NZIA	New Zealand Institute of Architects
OHS	Occupational Health & Safety
ONS	Office for National Statistics
OSB	Oriented Strand Board
OSB (2)	Over Site Board

PHC	Passive House Canada
PHINZ	Passive House Institute New Zealand
PHIUS	Passive House Institute US
PHPP	Passive House Planning Package
PLF	Personnel + Logistical + Financial
PP Fibres	Polypropylene Fibres
PPVC	Prefabricated Prefinished Volumetric Construction
PUD	Planned Unit Development
QA + QC	Quality Assurance + Quality Control
RAIA	Royal Australian Institute of Architects
RAIC	Royal Architectural Institute of Canada
RESPA	Real Estate Settlement Procedures Act
RIAI	Royal Institute of Architects of Ireland
RIBA	Royal Institute of British Architects
RICS	Royal Institute of Chartered Surveyors
SAP	Standard Assessment Procedure
SAPS	Stand Alone Power System
SEAI	Sustainable Energy Authority of Ireland
SEAOC	Structural Engineers Association of California
SFL	Structural Floor Level
SHGC	Solar Heat Gain Coefficient
SHS	Square Hollow Section
SHT	Smart Home Technology
SMART	Simple, Measurable, Attainable, Relevant & Time Based
SS	Stainless Steel
SUDS	Sustainable Urban Drainage System
SWMS	Safe Working Method Statement
SWO	Stop Work Order
TBM	Temporary Bench Mark
TER	Target Emission Rate
TILA	Truth in Lending Act

TPO	Tree Preservation Order
UHI	Urban Heat Islands
USGBC	The U.S. Green Building Council
VE	Value Engineering
VR	Virtual Reality
VOC	Volatile Organic Compounds
WiFi	Wireless Fidelity
WSUD	Water Sensitive Urban Design
ZOI	Zone of Influence

SERVICES ABBREVIATIONS

AAV	Air Admitance Valve
AC	Alternating Current
AFDD	Arc Fault Detection Device
AFIC	Ark Fault Circuit Interrupters
ASHP	Air Source Heat Pump
CBE	Circuit Breaker Enclosure
CCTV	Close Circuit Television
CCU	Customer Consumer Unit
CCU (2)	Customer Control Unit
Cpc	Circuit Protective Conductor
DB	Distribution Board
DC	Direct Current
DP	Down Pipe aka Down Spout
EMF	Electromotive Force
GFCB	Ground Fault Circuit Breaker
GFCI	Ground Fault Circuit Interruptor
GSHP	Ground Source Heat Pump
IP	Ingress Protection
IR	Infra Red
LED	Light-emiting diode
MCB	Miniature Circuit Breaker
MH	Manhole
PES	Phantom Energy Stealer

PV	Photovoltaics
RCB	Residual Current Device
RWP	Rain Water Pipe
SAP	Stand Alone Power
SC	Stop Cock
SPD	Surge Protection Device
SS	Stub Stack
SVP	Soil & Ventilation Pipe
TMV	Thermostatic Mixing Valves

EXCAVATION GLOSSARY

Arcing	An electrical current that jumps a gap.
Backfill	Material to refill an open excavation.
Batter Board	Board used to fix a known mark or nail to indicate a set out line for a trench.
Battering	The formed, faced angled wall of an excavation.
Benching	Horizontal stepping to the side walls of an excavation.
Biodegradable Shuttering/Formwork	Shuttering that decomposes and effectively disappears leaving a void.
Hurdle	The name given to the batter board and staked legs used to fix a set out line.
Overburden	Surface soil to be removed.
Reactive Soil	Soil that shrinks when dry and swells when wet.
Sacrificial Formwork	Formwork left in place on completion - often buried.
Safe Slope	A formed face to the side of an excavation to prevent earth slippage.
Sheet Piling	Vertical interlocking or continuous excavation support.
Shoring	To support or prop.
Shuttering	A mould used to form concrete structures.
Slurry Mix	Colloquial term for weak and high water content concrete mix.
Step Foundation	Multi-levelled foundation that steps down in line with a site slope.

Trench Shield   Steel pre-formed braces moved into a trench for support.

Zone of Influence   An area affected by external loads e.g. Vehicles excavated materials etc.

PROFESSIONAL ROLES

Acoustic Engineer	A consultant who assesses sound emanating from a building or methods of sound blocking through design.
Air Test Engineer	A consultant who tests air tightness or air permeability of buildings.
Appraiser	A person who assesses (determines) the fair market value of a property. They can be employed by a realtor, mortgage company or other party.
Architects	Architects plan and design buildings. Their qualifications and registration vary in different jurisdictions but they are generally considered the most qualified designers of buildings.
Architectural Technicians	Usually employed by architects or act as consultants offering the services of a draughtspersons (draftspersons). They can have a very wide-ranging technical role.
Builder/General Contractor/ Main or Principal Contractor	A person or organisation that acts as a builder to others and enters into formal contracts to carry out the work.
Builders Quantity Surveyor/ Estimator	A surveyor who acts for the building contractor. An estimator is a surveyor who calculates costs for projects.

Building Biologist	Evaluates toxins, health hazards and provides strategies to avoid products with VOCs etc.
Building Inspectors/Building Control Officers/District Surveyors/ Building Official/Municipal or Town Inspector.	An inspector of the building process who confirms on completion that the works conform with local building codes. They may be private consultants or public employees depending upon jurisdiction.
Building Services Engineer	A consultant and designer of building services, water, electrical, air conditioning etc.
Building Surveyor	A surveyor who can inspect and report on a project or take control of the design and contract administration.
Bushfire Assessors (BAL Assessments) AU/NZ	A consultant employed to report on the Bushfire Attack Level (BAL) of a property or area. They are only required in certain jurisdictions.
Civil Engineer	Engineer who designs or supervises large public works such as bridges, tunnels, roads etc.
Clerk of Works	A person employed by the client to check on site practice and works quality.
Contract Manager	A person in charge of more than one construction site. He is often employed by a Principal Contractor.
Contractor /Trade Contractor/ Specialist Contractor	A person or organization taking control of a package of work or single trade on site but is not in control of the site.
Conveyancer	A professional who acts for you in the purchase of a property. Solicitors often undertake this work.

Cost Engineer	Similar to a PQS although found more in US & Canada. Involved in cost control/forecasting and investment appraisal.
Cost Manager	Can be referred to as Quantity Surveyor offers timely advice on costs to the client and Principal Designer throughout the project.
Craftspeople/Tradespeople	Someone who is skilled in a single trade.
Design and Manage/Design and Build	A single organisation is contracted to deliver the design as well as the construction works.
Domestic Client	People who have construction carried out on a property they own.
Domestic Subcontractor/Supplier	Contractors solely selected by the Principal Contractor.
Draughtsperson (Draftsperson)	They create technical drawings either by hand or computer aided designs (CAD). They plan and design buildings but are not usually as highly qualified as architects.
Electrical Engineers	Design electrical power installations including lighting, transformers and telecommunications.
Energy Assessors	A registered consultant who assesses the energy usage of a property or design. This is a government requirement in some jurisdictions.
Estate Agents	They act for the seller of a property and advertise and negotiate the sale on the sellers behalf. They do not work for the purchaser.

Fire Officers/Fire Consultants	Fire Officers usually work for the Fire Service or Local Government and assess fire risk and fire vehicle access issues. Fire consultants do the same on behalf of the constructor.
General Operatives/Labourers/ Laborers US	Unskilled or Semi Skilled worker.
Geotechnical Engineer/Soil Engineer	Engineers who assess the ground supporting capacity of a site. They supply this information to Structural Engineers.
Heritage Advisor	A consultant who advises and prepares reports as part of the planning process. It is used to provide additional information on the heritage impact of your design in the locality. This is only necessary in designated 'heritage areas'.
Interior Decorator	A designer who helps you dress a finished product with fabrics and furnishings, wall coverings etc.
Interior Designer	A designer who only works on the interior finish and 'look' of the internal spaces. They can advise at the brief stage over location of doors, windows etc. to assist with the efficient use of space and furnishings.
"Land Surveyor/Consulting Surveyor and Planner /Licensed Land Surveyor/ Land Development & Subdivision Consultants "	A surveyor who carries out topographical surveys and often defines specific land parcels and levels. Some offer subdivision and development advice.
Landscape Architects	External environments, gardens, parks, streetscapes etc.
Lawyer	See Solicitor.

Main Contractor	The person or organisation in charge of the actual work. Named from someone who signed or issues contracts for signing.
Management Contracting	A site manager who commits to manage a project not supply the construction works. By agreement they can provide work packages though trade /specialist contractors and receive funds to pass over for payment.
Monitoring Surveyor	A surveyor who acts for a lender and monitors site progress for fund release.
Multi-Skilled	Someone who is skilled in more than one trade. Often not formally qualified in each trade.
Named Sub Contractor/Supplier	Contractors approved by the client as acceptable. The Principal Contractor does not have to use them as he takes responsibility for their work.
Nominated Sub Contractor/Supplier	Contractors that the client instructs the Principal Contractor to employ.
Owner-Builder	See Self-Builder.
Partnering	Partnering is where two or more organisations commit to collaborative relationships as a one off or as an ongoing long-term arrangement.
Party Wall Surveyor	A surveyor who advises on party wall and adjoining building matters. He can either work for the constructor or neighbour.
Planner/City Planner/Urban Planner/Town Planner	A planner can work as a private consultant or for a local authority or government body. They advise on land use, building use, density, planning refusal and appeals etc.

Principal Contractor	The person or organisation that acts as the controller of the construction process on a building site. Appointed to be in control of more than one contractor.
Principal Designer /CDM Co-ordinator	A manager and co-ordinator for the Construction Design and Management aspects of the H&S obligations of the client, design team and contractors. This is a necessary role in some jurisdictions.
Professional Quantity Surveyor (PQS)	A surveyor who calculates quantities of materials, prepares specifications and organizes and advises on the tender process. They often act in a project management role and offer aligned services such as H&S advice.
Project Manager	A person who manages a large single project or a few separate projects.
Property Finder	A professional who locates property, often off-market sales, and assists the purchaser. Some Estate Agents offer this service.
Right of Light Surveyor	A surveyor who calculates the amount of light that a building will receive or shade after construction.
Self-Builder	A person who builds for themselves usually for owner occupation. See Owner-Builder.
Solicitor/Barrister/Lawyer	The catchall term is Lawyer. They advise and represent clients in a variety of legal matters.
Statutory Contractor/Infrastructure Supplier	Contractor qualified to work on statutory services in public and private places such as roads, sewers etc. Often a monopoly.

Structural Engineer	Engineers who design the structure of a building.
Sub-Contractor/Subs/Subbie	A contractor who agrees a contract with the General Contractor for a section of work.
Tree Officers, Species and Habitat Assessors, Botanists	Consultants who can work for local government or act as consultants to constructors.
Valuation Surveyor	Surveyors who recommend a fair market value for a property. They can work for vendors or purchasers but their main clients are either lenders who want an independent valuation for lending purposes or insurance companies for insurance / replacement values.
VDC Project Manager/BIM	Virtual Design-to-Construction Manager & Building Information Management Manager. A designer who models the whole concept-to-occupation process through digital representation.
Vendor/Seller	Seller of a property.
Worker/Operative	Someone who works under the instruction of a contractor/builder.

INDEX

A

Active solar, 4
Air Test, 166
Air Source Heat Pumps, 5

B

Baseboard & Trim, 178
Benching & Battering, 95
Boundary Management, 57
Bricks, 131
Building Information Modelling (BIM), 75

C

Chimneys, 158
Coefficient of Performance, 6
Concrete Testing, 123
Curtain Walls 153

D

Doors, 177
Diversity, 111
Drains, 133
Drylining, 173

E

Electricity, 100
Equality of Access 173
Excavations, 91

F

Finished Floor Levels, 76
Fire, 45
Floors, 143
Foundations, 125

G

Gas, 107
Glass, 157
Goal Gradients, 23
Ground Source Heat Pumps, 5

H

Heating, 110

I

International Building Code, 83
International Residential Code, 83

K

Kitchens, 179

L

Landscaping, 9
Laser Level, 77
Legionella, 108-109
Letters of Intent, 203
Locks, 158
Low Energy Designs, 3

M

Mechanical Services, 5
Mechanical Ventilation Heat Recovery (MVHR), 6
Modern Methods of Construction(MMC), 37

N

National Building Code, 83

O

Office Organization, xii

P

Passive Solar, 4
Ponds, 3
Project Manager, 20
Punch List, 60
Purchase Orders, 66-67
Photovoltaics (PV), 105

Q

Quality Assurance, 62
Quality Control, 58,62

R

Rainwater Harvesting, 164
Reduction Creep, 32
Retaining Walls 132
Roofs, 159
Right Angle, 73
Risk, 30

S

Safe Method Working Statement (SWMS), 48
Schedule of Work, 21
Scope Creep, 31
Setting Out, 72
Site Survey 74

Smart Home Technology (SHT), 7-9,115
Stairs, 175-6

T

Tenders, 194
Top Soil, 74
Toxic Contamination, 121

U

U-Values, 86,147
Urban Heat Islands, 10

W

Walls, 147
Water Management, 7,108
Wardrobes, 180
Wildfires, 149
Windows, 150

Z

Zero Carbon Emissions, 2
Zone Permit, 84

ABOUT THE AUTHOR

Born into a building family, Philip always had his eye on the trade. After leaving school, he joined a prestigious building company and went on to become a qualified building surveyor and a Member of the Chartered Institute of Building (MCIOB). Philip has acted as a consultant across the US as well as partnering with US based companies to develop projects in the Caribbean. He has completed projects in the UK, Ireland, Europe, North Africa and Australia. At the invitation of the US government, he has spoken to and met educational and trade association groups across the US regarding construction training and Modern Methods of Construction. Philip has worked on numerous 'special' new build residential projects and on many public & government buildings, railway infrastructure, retail, commercial, clinical & medical facilities and apartment blocks.

Over the years, Philip's company has won awards from the Royal Institute of British Architects, the Civic Trust, the Department of the Environment and the National House Builders Council (NHBC). He is an experienced public speaker and shares his take on current building matters and related topics. He has also supported and served as a board member of charities promoting training in the construction industry for young people and mid-career changers.

First and foremost, Philip is a builder.

Philip can be contacted directly at philip@abuilderscompanion.com

TAKE-AWAYS

'My policy on cake is pro having it and pro eating it'.
— *Boris Johnson*

These are listed in no particular order, as events can occur in any order, and any of the following tips may set you off on a train of thought. Please send me your tips to be included in a future edition.

- Always plan accessible isolation points
- Group and label isolator points together for all kitchen appliances
- Have a single switch to turn off all your office appliances
- Check what screw or fixing is required for where… the wrong screw can lead to unwanted consequences
- Measure out doors and windows to ensure the trim is full all the way around
- All steps on a staircase must be equal and where possible the going and rises on different staircases should all match
- Ask plumbers to use a single color pipe, particularly where pipes are visible or in cupboards
- Set out locks on external doors to be effective as far as strength against burglary
- All locks on windows should work from a single key
- Datum levels are key and should be clearly visible on site; no guesses
- Thermal (aka cold) bridging—be vigilant for items that close the gap
- Unplanned holes in structure cause air leakage problems and waste energy
- How big a gap between door and floor?
- Rain water downspouts and drain outlets all fall away from the house
- Never be afraid to put an instruction in writing and try to value it as you proceed… this is to keep an eye on budgets

- Be careful of where responsibilities overlap, electricians and plumbers in particular
- Always tell the designers if you are building things differently to their design
- Make sure door handles are set back, with locks that do not catch fingers on the frame or stop
- Consider the most appropriate drywall sheet in any given situation
- Drill services through the center zone of a joist
- Issue plastic laminated covered plans to site operatives
- Issue details to tradesmen for specific required details—do not rely on their usual solution
- If having a special tilt garage door, check weight of cladding material to avoid excessively large motors
- Check the weight capabilities of sliding and bi-folding gear before order is placed, to ensure it is adequate
- Keep the site safe, with secure hoardings
- Keep OH&S signage and information visible
- Insist workers wear Hi Viz clothes and appropriate footwear, goggles, etc.
- Just telling people something is the least efficient method of communicating. Give them a specification or drawing
- Have secure tool storage on site but do not guarantee tool security to contractors
- Place temporary 'service positions' in a place where they will be long term
- Never ask someone to do something that you would not safely do yourself
- All ladders and platforms on site must be safe to use
- Ventilation must be planned; do not rely on random acts of poor workmanship
- Pay attention where works cross-over, such as around door and window openings, especially where they may be subject to wind and rain
- Try to reduce, as far as possible, opening or penetrations in slabs or roofs
- Always run the services inside wall partitions in straight zones
- Will future purchasers of your home want it to be eco-friendly?
- Understand the difference between keyed alike and master keys
- Understand the importance of drips to coping stones and window cills ... the Victorians can still teach us a lesson
- Does it matter *who is to blame*, as the owner-builder will always end up footing the bill

- Check the 'setting out' of all services before the wall or floors are fitted. Get a drawing and check each and every point
- When you supply specialist fittings to plumbers/electricians, pay particular note of who accepts them from you. Confirm they will take responsibility for all the parts (and bits of the parts) supplied

DO YOU FEEL 'COMPANIONABLE'?

I hope you enjoyed The Builder's Companion Book 2, Start Building to Certificate of Occupancy. Can you please take a moment to share your review on the site you purchased this book and on social media (anywhere between two words and as many as you like) would be very helpful to me and benefit other owner–builder's to find the book.

Do you know of someone else with an interest in home building?

Have you thought of sending them a copy of the book or e-book?

I would be pleased if we can get the book out there.

Just drop me a line at philip@abuilderscompanion.com letting me know what you think and I will personally respond.

Everyone needs a building buddy or …The Builder's Companion.

Made in the USA
Las Vegas, NV
24 October 2023

79627911R00149